# The Vedas Or Books Of Holy

# Knowledge

**Charles F. Horne**

# Kessinger Publishing's Rare Reprints

## Thousands of Scarce and Hard-to-Find Books on These and other Subjects!

- Americana
- Ancient Mysteries
- Animals
- Anthropology
- Architecture
- Arts
- Astrology
- Bibliographies
- Biographies & Memoirs
- Body, Mind & Spirit
- Business & Investing
- Children & Young Adult
- Collectibles
- Comparative Religions
- Crafts & Hobbies
- Earth Sciences
- Education
- Ephemera
- Fiction
- Folklore
- Geography
- Health & Diet
- History
- Hobbies & Leisure
- Humor
- Illustrated Books
- Language & Culture
- Law
- Life Sciences
- Literature
- Medicine & Pharmacy
- Metaphysical
- Music
- Mystery & Crime
- Mythology
- Natural History
- Outdoor & Nature
- Philosophy
- Poetry
- Political Science
- Science
- Psychiatry & Psychology
- Reference
- Religion & Spiritualism
- Rhetoric
- Sacred Books
- Science Fiction
- Science & Technology
- Self-Help
- Social Sciences
- Symbolism
- Theatre & Drama
- Theology
- Travel & Explorations
- War & Military
- Women
- Yoga
- *Plus Much More!*

**We kindly invite you to view our catalog list at:
http://www.kessinger.net**

# THE RIG-VEDA

*"The Veda, I feel convinced, will occupy scholars for centuries to come, and will take and maintain forever its position as the most ancient of books in the library of mankind."*

— F. MAX MULLER.

# THE RIG-VEDA

## (INTRODUCTION)

THE name "Rig" means a song of praise, "Veda" means holy knowledge; so we have here a book of holy knowledge, made up of hymns. There are three other Hymn Vedas made up of similar songs, but they are of later date than the Rig, and their hymns are to some extent borrowed from it. Hence the Rig stands out as both the oldest and the most important. A Hindu tradition represents the Vedas as being as old as creation; and in accordance with this the reputed author of each hymn is not said to have composed it, but to have first "seen" it; that is, had it revealed to him. The Hindus have no records of ancient chronology whatever, yet even their modern scholars still gravely claim for the Rig-Veda an antiquity of from eight to twelve thousand years! European scholars smile at this. They can trace the Rig back to about 1200 B.C., and they are inclined to set its earliest possible beginnings at about 2000 B.C.

The Rig consists of over a thousand hymns, divided into ten Mandalas, or books. The first of these Mandalas is the longest and seemingly the oldest. Its hymns address only the very primitive gods: Indra, the god of the sky; Agni, the god of fire; and their immediate attendants, such as the sun-god, the wind-god, and those extremely interesting old heroes, the Maruts, or storm-gods. Professor Muller has made a special study of the Maruts as being perhaps the most primitive gods of all. In the hymns to them the growth and change of the religious spirit can be sharply traced. So our volume gives many of the Marut hymns. The earliest Aryan conception that there were outside powers to fear and to appease may well have been connected with the menace of the gathering thunder-storm.

But if the Maruts came first, in the primeval Aryan worship, then before the Rig was formed they had been already outranked by the broader conception of Indra, a general god of the weather, commanding the heavens in all their various moods toward man. Between Indra and the Maruts there is almost a clash of powers; and the doubt as to which should be addressed and placated shows often in the mind of the priestly singers. Indeed the favorite of the priests was neither of these warlike forces, but that other and more pacific deity, Agni. They have placed his hymns first in each of the ten Mandalas.

After the first and oldest Mandala, the Rig presents seven Mandalas containing the hymns preserved, and perhaps composed, by seven priestly families. Each of these books received the family name. The ninth Mandala contains only hymns to Soma. Soma was the intoxicating drink of the early Hindus, a milk-like, fermented liquor, which, because of its inspiring effect upon its devotees, seems to have been elevated to the full rank of a god. Not only did the Hindus use the beverage in their religious sacrifices, not only did they offer it to the gods, but they made it the subject of sacrifice and worship.

The tenth Mandala of the Rig seems, like the first, a collection from many sources. But it is a collection of later days. Long after the first nine books had become holy, there must have arisen new poems which seemed worthy to rank with them. Moreover, an effort may have been made to save such older songs as before had not been included in the holy books; and in rescuing these the priests were less particular than before as to the religious spirit of the poem. At any rate, there are in the tenth Mandala several poems which we would scarcely rank as hymns. They seem survivals of a looser verse. Yet the tenth Mandala contains also some of the most celebrated hymns of the entire Rig. Among these are the Creation Hymn, interesting in its resemblance to the Biblical account, and the hymn which we print last as perhaps the most impressive and profound of all, the Address to the Unknown God.

One other point of rather striking interest about these ancient poems is that several of them are attributed to woman authors. In this they are unique among the sacred books of the Farther East. Our Bible knows of the song of Miriam and of the prophetess Deborah; but no other Eastern literature presents the names or works of female writers of anything like a similar antiquity. Woman's position among these earliest Aryans seems to have been one of trust and honor. The following translations include two of these women's poems. The first of these may well hold our attention as being apparently the oldest piece of feminine literature that has survived the ages. Legend represents its opening stanzas as being actually composed by the princess Lopamudra, who wedded a brahmin sage and clung to him "like a shadow" through all his abstraction and self-mortification. As the poem appears in the first Mandala, we may roughly assign it to about the year 2000 B.C. Other poetesses of the Rig are the princess Visvavará, the goddess, or rather wife of a god, Idrani, and the mystic Vac, woman, goddess, or the personification of the power of words. Vac's noble hymn, which we give here, has been at least as much translated and discussed as even the Address to the Unknown God.

# THE RIG-VEDA

## BOOK I.— HYMN 1 [1]

1. I worship by hymns Agni, the high-priest of the sacrifice, the deity, the sacrificial priest who presents oblations to the deities and is the possessor of great riches.

2. May Agni, lauded by the ancient and modern Rishis, conduct the deities hither (*i.e.,* in this sacrifice).

3. Through Agni, the worshiper comes by wealth which multiplies daily, which is the source of fame and which secures heroes.

4. O Agni, the sacrifice, around which thou residest, is unimpeded and reaches the celestials in heaven.

5. May Agni, the presenter of oblations, the attainer of success in works, ever truthful, highly illustrious for many noble deeds, divine, come hither with the celestials.

6. Whatever good, O Agni, thou mayest confer upon the giver of oblations, that, indeed, O Angiras, belongs to thee.

7. Bowing unto thee mentally, O Agni, we approach thee daily, both morning and evening.

8. Thee, the radiant, the protector of sacrifices unobstructed by Rakshasas, the perpetual illuminator of truth and increasing in thine own room.

9. Like unto a father to his son, O Agni, be easily accessible unto us; be ever present with us for our well-being.[2]

## BOOK I.— HYMN 2 [3]

1. Come hither, O Vayu, thou beautiful one! These Somas are ready; drink of them; hear our call!

[1] The "Rishi," or holy sage who composed the first three hymns, is said to be Madhuchhandas, a descendant of the most ancient and celebrated teacher or god, Vaisvamitrā.

[2] This translation is by the modern Hindu poet, Manmutha Dutt.

[3] Vayu is the wind, a sort of attendant deity of Indra. Mitra and

2. O Vayu, the praisers celebrate thee with hymns, they who know the feast-days, and have prepared the Soma.

3. O Vayu, thy satisfying stream goes to the worshiper, wide-reaching, to the Soma-draught.

4. O Indra and Vayu, these libations of Soma are poured out; come hither for the sake of our offerings, for the drops of Soma long for you.

5. O Indra and Vayu, you perceive the libations, you who are rich in booty; come then quickly hither!

6. O Vayu and Indra, come near to the work of the sacrificer quick; thus is my prayer, O ye men!

7. I call Mitra, endowed with holy strength, and Varuna, who destroys all enemies; who both fulfil a prayer accompanied by fat offerings.

8. On the right way, O Mitra and Varuna, you have obtained great wisdom, you who increase the right and adhere to the right;

9. These two sages, Mitra and Varuna, the mighty, wide-ruling, give us efficient strength.[4]


## BOOK I.—HYMN 3 [5]

1. Aswins, cherishers of pious deeds, having outstretched hands for accepting the oblation, long-armed, desire for sacrificial viands.

2. Aswins, of many acts, guides of devotion, endowed with intellect, accept our eulogistic words with unaverted minds.

3. Aswins, destroyers of diseases, shorn of falsehood, leaders in the van of heroes, come to the mixed libations of Soma, extracted and placed on lopped Kus'a-grass.

Varuna seem special forms of fire, forms more fierce than Agni, the hearth-fire. Later they become day and night.

[4] Translated by Max Muller.

[5] The Aswins are two sons of the sun. They are warlike heroes and are also healing gods, or physicians. The Viswadevas are specifically a class of lesser gods, somewhat like guardian-spirits of men; but the term is often used collectively to include all gods. Saraswati is the goddess of speech, a truly feminine deity.

4. Indra of variegated splendor, come hither; these libations, ever pure and extracted by fingers, are seeking thee.

5. Indra, drawn by the devotion of the sacrificer and invoked by the intelligent priest, come hither and accept the prayers of the priest as he offers the libation.

6. Indra, having tawny horses, come hither speedily, to accept the prayers of the priest; in this sacrifice of extracted Soma-juice, accept our proffered food.

7. Viswadevas, protectors, supporters of men, granters of sacrificial rewards, come to the extracted Soma-juice of the worshiper.

8. May Viswadevas, the bestowers of rain, come speedily to the libation, as the rays of the sun come diligently to the days.

9. May Viswadevas, who are exempt from deterioration, omniscient, shorn of malice, givers of wealth, partake of this sacrifice.

10. May Saraswati, the purifier, the giver of food, the bestower of wealth in the shape of sacrificial fruits, seek viands in our sacrificial rite.

11. Saraswati, the inspirer of truthful words, the instructress of the right-minded, has accepted our sacrifice.

12. Saraswati makes manifest by her deeds a huge river, and in her own form enlightens all her undertakings.[6]


## BOOK I.— HYMN 6 [7]

### To Indra and the Maruts (the Storm-gods) [8]

1. Those who stand around him while he moves on, harness the bright red steed; the lights in heaven shine forth.

[6] Translated by Manmutha Dutt.

[7] The hymns that follow are all translated by Prof. Muller.

[8] The poet begins with a somewhat abrupt description of a sunrise. Indra is taken as the god of the bright day, whose steed is the sun, and whose companions are the Maruts, or the storm-gods. *Arushá*, meaning originally "red," is used as a proper name of the horse or of the rising sun, though it occurs more frequently as the name of the red horses or flames of Agni, the god of fire, and also of the morning

2. They harness to the chariot on each side his (Indra's) two favorite bays, the brown, the bold, who can carry the hero.

3. Thou who createst light where there was no light, and form, O men! where there was no form, hast been born together with the dawns.

4. Thereupon they (the Maruts), according to their wont, assumed again the form of new-born babes, taking their sacred name.

5. Thou, O Indra, with the swift Maruts who break even through the stronghold hast found even in their hiding-place the bright ones (days or clouds).

6. The pious singers (the Maruts) have, after their own mind, shouted toward the giver of wealth, the great, the glorious Indra.

7. Mayest thou, host of the Maruts, be verily seen coming together with Indra, the fearless: you are both happy-making, and of equal splendor.

8. With the beloved hosts of Indra, with the blameless, hasting Maruts, the sacrificer cries aloud.

9. From yonder, O traveler (Indra), come hither, or from the light of heaven; the singers all yearn for it;

10. Or we ask Indra for help from here, or from heaven, or from above the earth, or from the great sky.

## BOOK I.— HYMN 19

### To Agni and the Maruts

1. Thou art called forth to this fair sacrifice for a draught of milk; with the Maruts come hither, O Agni!

light. In our passage, *Arushá*, a substantive, meaning the "red of the morning," has taken *bradhná* as an adjective, *bradhná* meaning, as far as can be made out, "bright" in general, though, as it is especially applied to the Soma-juice, perhaps "bright-brown" or "yellow." Names of color are difficult to translate from one language into another, for their shades vary, and withdraw themselves from sharp definition. We meet with this difficulty again and again in the Veda.

2. No god indeed, no mortal, is beyond the might of thee, the mighty one; with the Maruts come hither, O Agni!

3. They who know of the great sky, the Visve Devas without guile; with those Maruts come hither, O Agni!

4. The strong ones who sing their song, unconquerable by force; with the Maruts come hither, O Agni!

5. They who are brilliant, of terrible designs, powerful, and devourers of foes; with the Maruts come hither, O Agni!

6. They who in heaven are enthroned as gods, in the light of the firmament; with the Maruts come hither, O Agni!

7. They who toss the clouds across the surging sea; with the Maruts come hither, O Agni!

8. They who shoot with their darts (lightnings) across the sea with might; with the Maruts come hither, O Agni!

9. I pour out to thee for the early draught the sweet juice of Soma; with the Maruts come hither, O Agni!


## BOOK I.— HYMN 37

### To the Maruts

1. Sing forth, O Kanvas, to the sportive host of your Maruts, brilliant on their chariots, and unscathed —

2. They who were born together, self-luminous, with the spotted deer (the clouds), the spears, the daggers, the glittering ornaments.

3. I hear their whips, almost close by, when they crack them in their hands; they gain splendor on their way.

4. Sing forth the god-given prayer to the wild host of your Maruts, endowed with terrible vigor and strength.

5. Celebrate the bull among the cows (the storm among the clouds), for it is the sportive host of the Maruts; he grew as he tasted the rain.

6. Who, O ye men, is the strongest among you here, ye shakers of heaven and earth, when you shake them like the hem of a garment?

7. At your approach the son of man holds himself down; the gnarled cloud fled at your fierce anger.

8. They at whose racings the earth, like a hoary king, trembles for fear on their ways, .

9. Their birth is strong indeed: there is strength to come forth from their mother; nay, there is vigor twice enough for it.

10. And these sons, the singers, stretched out the fences in their racings; the cows had to walk knee-deep.

11. They cause this long and broad unceasing rain to fall on their ways.

12. O Maruts, with such strength as yours, you have caused men to tremble, you have caused the mountains to tremble.

13. As the Maruts pass along, they talk together on the way: does any one hear them?

14. Come fast on your quick steeds! there are worshipers for you among the Kanvas: may you well rejoice among them.

15. Truly there is enough for your rejoicing. We always are their servants, that we may live even the whole of life.

## BOOK I.— HYMN 38

### To the Maruts

1. What then now? When will you take us as a dear father takes his son by both hands, O ye gods, for whom the sacred grass has been trimmed?

2. Where now? On what errand of yours are you going, in heaven, not on earth? Where are your cows sporting?

3. Where are your newest favors, O Maruts? Where the blessings? Where all delights?

4. If you, sons of Prisni, were mortals, and your praiser an immortal —

5. Then never should your praiser be unwelcome, like a deer in pasture grass, nor should he go on the path of Yama.

6. Let not one sin after another, difficult to be conquered, overcome us; may it depart together with greed.

7. Truly they are terrible and powerful; even to the desert the Rudriyas bring rain that is never dried up.

8. The lightning lows like a cow; it follows as a mother follows after her young, when the shower of the Maruts has been let loose.

9. Even by day the Maruts create darkness with the water-bearing cloud, when they drench the earth.

10. Then from the shouting of the Maruts over the whole space of the earth, men reeled forward.

11. Maruts on your strong-hoofed, never-wearying steeds go after those bright ones (the clouds), which are still locked up.

12. May your fellies be strong, the chariots, and their horses; may your reins be well-fashioned.

13. Speak forth forever with thy voice to praise the Lord of prayer, Agni, who is like a friend, the bright one.

14. Fashion a hymn in thy mouth! Expand like the cloud! Sing a song of praise.

15. Worship the host of the Maruts, the terrible, the glorious, the musical. May they be magnified here among us.


## BOOK I.— HYMN 39

### To the Maruts

1. When you thus from afar cast forward your measure, like a blast of fire, through whose wisdom is it, through whose design? To whom do you go, to whom, ye shakers of the earth?

2. May your weapons be firm to attack, strong also to withstand. May yours be the more glorious power, nor that of the deceitful mortal.

3. When you overthrow what is firm, O ye men, and whirl about what is heavy, you pass through the trees of the earth, through the clefts of the rocks.

4. No real foe of yours is known in heaven, nor on earth, ye devourers of foes! May power be yours, together with your race! O Rudras, can it be defied?

5. They make the rocks tremble, they tear asunder the kings of the forest. Come on, Maruts, like madmen, ye gods, with your whole tribe.

6. You have harnessed the spotted deer to your chariots, a red one draws as leader; even the earth listened at your approach, and men were frightened.

7. O Rudras, we quickly desire your help for our race. Come now to us with help, as of yore; thus now for the sake of the frightened Kanva.

8. Whatever fiend, roused by you or roused by men, attacks us, deprive him of power, of strength, and of your favors.

9. For you, chasing and wise Maruts, have wholly protected Kanva. Come to us, Maruts, with your whole favors, as lightnings go in quest of the rain.

10. Bounteous givers, you carry whole strength, whole power, ye shakers of the world. Send, O Maruts, against the wrathful enemy of the poets an enemy, like an arrow.

## BOOK I.—HYMN 64

### To the Maruts

1. For the manly host, the joyful, the wise, for the Maruts bring thou, O Nodhas,[9] a pure offering. I prepare songs, like as a handy priest, wise in his mind, prepares the water, mighty at sacrifices.

2. They are born, the tall bulls of Dyu (heaven), the manly youths of Rudra, the divine, the blameless, pure, and bright like suns; scattering raindrops, full of terrible designs, like giants.

3. The youthful Rudras, they who never grow old, the slayers of the demon, have grown irresistible like mountains. They throw down with their strength all beings, even the strongest, on earth and in heaven.

4. They deck themselves with glittering ornaments for a marvelous show; on their chests they fastened gold chains

9 Here the singer Nodhas addresses himself.

for beauty; the spears on their shoulders pound to pieces; they were born together by themselves, the men of Dyu.

5. They who confer power, the roarers, the devourers of foes, they made winds and lightnings by their powers. The shakers milk the heavenly udders (clouds), they sprinkle the earth all round with milk (rain).

6. The bounteous Maruts pour forth water, mighty at sacrifices, the fat milk of the clouds. They seem to lead about the powerful horse, the cloud, to make it rain; they milk the thundering, unceasing spring.

7. Mighty they are, powerful, of beautiful splendor, strong in themselves like mountains, yet swiftly gliding along; you chew up forests, like wild elephants, when you have assumed your powers among the red flames.

8. Like lions they roar, the wise Maruts; they are handsome like gazelles, the all-knowing. By night with their spotted deer (rain-clouds) and with their spears (lightnings) they rouse the companions together, they whose ire through strength is like the ire of serpents.

9. You who march in companies, the friends of man, heroes, whose ire through strength is like the ire of serpents, salute heaven and earth! On the seats on your chariots, O Maruts, the lightning stands, visible like light.

10. All-knowing, surrounded with wealth, endowed with powers, singers, men of endless prowess, armed with strong rings, they, the archers, have taken the arrow in their fists.

11. The Maruts who with the golden tires of their wheels increase the rain, stir up the clouds like wanderers on the road. They are brisk, indefatigable, they move by themselves; they throw down what is firm, the Maruts with their brilliant spears make everything to reel.

12. We invoke with prayer the offspring of Rudra, the brisk, the pure, the worshipful, the active. Cling for happiness-sake to the strong company of the Maruts, the chasers of the sky, the powerful, the impetuous.

13. The mortal whom ye, Maruts, protected, he indeed surpasses people in strength through your protection. He

carries off booty with his horses, treasures with his men; he acquires honorable wisdom, and he prospers.

14. Give, O Maruts, to our lords strength glorious, invincible in battle, brilliant, wealth-acquiring, praiseworthy, known to all men. Let us foster our kith and kin during a hundred winters.

15. Will you then, O Maruts, grant unto us wealth, durable, rich in men, defying all onslaughts? — wealth a hundred and a thousandfold, always increasing? — May he who is rich in prayers (the host of the Maruts) come early and soon!

## BOOK I.— HYMN 86

### To the Maruts

1. O Maruts, that man in whose dwelling you drink the Soma, ye mighty sons of heaven, he indeed has the best guardians.

2. You who are propitiated either by sacrifices or from the prayers of the sage, hear the call, O Maruts!

3. Aye, the powerful man to whom you have granted a sage, he will live in a stable rich in cattle.

4. On the altar of this strong man here, Soma is poured out in daily sacrifices; praise and joy are sung.

5. To him let the mighty Maruts listen, to him who surpasses all men, as the flowing rain-clouds pass over the sun.

6. For we, O Maruts, have sacrificed at many harvests, through the mercies of the swift gods (the storm-gods).

7. May that mortal be blessed, O chasing Maruts, whose offerings you carry off.

8. You take notice either of the sweat of him who praises you, ye men of true strength, or of the desire of the suppliant.

9. O ye of true strength, make this manifest with might! strike the fiend with your lightning!

10. Hide the hideous darkness, destroy every tusky fiend. Make the light which we long for!

## BOOK I.— HYMN 87

### To the Maruts

1. Endowed with exceeding vigor and power, the singers, the never-flinching, the immovable, the impetuous, the most beloved and most manly, have decked themselves with their glittering ornaments, a few only, like the heavens with the stars.

2. When you have seen your way through the clefts, like birds, O Maruts, on whatever road it be, then the casks (clouds) on your chariots trickle everywhere, and you pour out the honey-like fatness (the rain) for him who praises you.

3. At their racings the earth shakes, as if broken, when on the heavenly paths they harness their deer for victory. They the sportive, the roaring, with bright spears, the shakers of the clouds have themselves glorified their greatness.

4. That youthful company of the Maruts, with their spotted horses, moves by itself; hence it exercises lordship, invested with powers. Thou indeed art true; thou searchest out sin; thou art without blemish. Therefore the manly host will help this prayer.

5. We speak after the kind of our old father, our tongue goes forth at the sight of the Soma: when the singers (the Maruts) had joined Indra in deed, then only they took their holy names;

6. These Maruts, armed with beautiful rings, obtained splendors for their glory, they obtained rays, and men to celebrate them; nay, armed with daggers, speeding along, and fearless, they found the beloved domain of the Maruts.

## BOOK I.— HYMN 88

### To the Maruts

1. Come hither, Maruts, on your chariots charged with lightning, resounding with beautiful songs, stored with spears, and winged with horses! Fly to us like birds, with your best food, you mighty ones!

2. They come gloriously on their red, or, it may be, on their tawny horses which hasten their chariots. He who holds the axe is brilliant like gold; with the tire of the chariot they have struck the earth.

3. On your bodies there are daggers for beauty; may they stir up our minds as they stir up the forests. For yourselves, O well-born Maruts, the vigorous among you shake the stone for distilling Soma.

4. Days went round you and came back, O hawks, back to this prayer, and to this sacred rite; the Gotamas making prayer with songs, pushed up the lid of the well (the cloud) for to drink.

5. No such hymn was ever known as this which Gotama sounded for you, O Maruts, when he saw you on golden wheels, wild boars rushing about with iron tusks.

6. This comforting speech rushes sounding toward you, like the speech of a suppliant: it rushed freely from our hands as our speeches are wont to do.

## BOOK I.— HYMN 165

### To the Maruts and Indra [10]

#### The Prologue

The sacrificer speaks:

1. To what splendor do the Maruts all equally cling, they who are of the same age, and dwell in the same nest? With

[10] It would seem as if the ten verses, from 3 to 12, formed an independent poem, which was intended to show the divine power of the Maruts. That their divine power was sometimes denied, and that Indra's occasional contempt of them was well known to the Vedic poets, will become evident from other hymns. This dialogue seems, therefore, to have been distinctly intended to show that, in spite of occasional misunderstandings between the Maruts and the all-powerful Indra, Indra himself had fully recognized their power and accepted their friendship. If we suppose that this dialogue was repeated at sacrifices in honor of the Maruts, or that possibly it was acted by two parties, one representing Indra, the other the Maruts and their followers, then the two verses in the beginning and the three at the end ought to be placed in the mouth of the actual sacrificer, whoever he was. He begins

what thoughts? — from whence are they come? Do these heroes sing forth their own strength, wishing for wealth?

2. Whose prayers have the youths accepted? Who has turned the Maruts to his own sacrifice? By what strong desire may we arrest them, they who float through the air like hawks?

*The Dialogue*

The Maruts speak:

3. From whence, O Indra, dost thou come alone, thou who art mighty? O lord of men, what has thus happened to thee? Thou greetest us when thou comest together with us, the bright Maruts. Tell us then, thou with thy bay horses, what thou hast against us!

4. The sacred songs are mine; mine are the prayers; sweet are the libations! My strength rises; my thunderbolt is hurled forth. They call for me; the hymns yearn for me. Here are my horses; they carry me hither.

The Maruts speak:

5. From thence, in company with our strong friends, having adorned our bodies, we now harness our fallow deer with all our might; for, Indra, according to custom, thou hast come to be with us.

Indra speaks:

6. Where, O Maruts, was that custom with you, when you left me alone in the killing of Ahi? I indeed am terrible, powerful, strong; I escaped from the blows of every enemy.

The Maruts speak:

7. Thou hast achieved much with us as companions. With

by asking, Who has attracted the Maruts to his sacrifice, and by what act of praise and worship can they be delighted? Then follows the dialogue in honor of the Maruts, and after it the sacrificer asks again, "Who has magnified the Maruts, *i.e.*, have not we magnified them?" and he implores them to grant him their friendship in recognition of his acts of worship. If then we suppose that the dialogue was the work of Mândârya Mânya, the fourteenth verse, too, would lose something of its obscurity. Coming from the mouth of the actual sacrificer, it would mean, "the wisdom, or the poetical power, of Mânya has brought us to this, has induced us to do this, *i.e.*, to perform this dialogue of Mânya, so that he, Mânya, should assist, as a poet assists the priest at a sacrifice."

equal valor, O hero! let us achieve then many things, O thou most powerful, O Indra! whatever we, O Maruts, wish with our mind.

Indra speaks:

8. I slew Vritra, O Maruts, with Indra's might, having grown powerful through my own vigor; I, who hold the thunderbolt in my arms, have made these all-brilliant waters to flow freely for man.

The Maruts speak:

9. Nothing, O mighty lord, is strong before thee: no one is known among the gods like unto thee. No one who is now born comes near, no one who has been born. Do what thou wilt do, thou who art grown so strong.

Indra speaks:

10. Almighty strength be mine alone, whatever I may do, daring in my heart; for I indeed, O Maruts, am known as terrible: of all that I threw down, I, Indra, am the lord.

Indra speaks:

11. O Maruts, now your praise has pleased me, the glorious hymn which you have made for me, ye men! — for me, for Indra, for the joyful hero, as friends for a friend, for your own sake, and by your own efforts.

Indra speaks:

12. Truly, there they are, shining toward me, bringing blameless glory, bringing food. O Maruts, wherever I have looked for you, you have appeared to me in bright splendor: appear to me also now!

### The Epilogue

The sacrificer speaks:

13. Who has magnified you here, O Maruts? Come hither, O friends, toward your friends. Ye brilliant Maruts, welcoming these prayers, be mindful of these my rites.

14. The wisdom of Mânya has brought us hither, that he should help as the poet helps the performer of a sacrifice: turn hither quickly! Maruts, on to the sage! the singer has recited these prayers for you.

15. May this your praise, O Maruts, this song of Mân-dârya, the son of Mâna, the poet, bring offspring for ourselves with food. May we have an invigorating autumn, with quickening rain.

## BOOK I.— HYMN 166

### To the Maruts

1. Let us now proclaim for the robust host, for the herald of the powerful Indra, their ancient greatness! O ye strong-voiced Maruts, you heroes, prove your powers on your march, as with a torch, as with a sword!

2. Like parents bringing a dainty to their own son, the wild Maruts play playfully at the sacrifices. The Rudras reach the worshiper with their protection; strong in themselves, they do not fail the sacrificer.

3. For him to whom the immortal guardians have given fulness of wealth, and who is himself a giver of oblations, the Maruts, who gladden men with the milk of rain, pour out, like friends, many clouds.

4. You who have stirred up the clouds with might, your horses rushed forth, self-guided. All beings who dwell in houses are afraid of you; your march is brilliant with your spears thrust forth.

5. When they whose march is terrible have caused the rocks to tremble, or when the manly Maruts have shaken the back of heaven, then every lord of the forest fears at your racing, each shrub flies out of your way, whirling like char-iot-wheels.

6. You, O terrible Maruts, whose ranks are never broken, favorably fulfil our prayer! Wherever your glory-toothed lightning bites, it crunches cattle, like a well-aimed bolt.

7. The Maruts whose gifts are firm, whose bounties are never ceasing, who do not revile, and who are highly praised at the sacrifices, they sing their song for to drink the sweet juice: they know the first manly deeds of the hero Indra.

8. The man whom you have guarded, O Maruts, shield

him with hundredfold strongholds from injury and mischief
— the man whom you, O fearful, powerful singers, protect
from reproach in the prosperity of his children.

9. On your chariots, O Maruts, there are all good things,
strong weapons are piled up clashing against each other.
When you are on your journeys, you carry the rings on your
shoulders, and your axle turns the two wheels at once.

10. In their manly arms there are many good things, on
their chests golden chains, flaring ornaments, on their shoulders speckled deer-skins, on their fellies sharp edges; as birds
spread their wings, they spread out splendors behind.

11. They, mighty by might, all-powerful powers, visible
from afar like the heavens with the stars, sweet-toned, soft-
tongued singers with their mouths, the Maruts, united with
Indra, shout all around.

12. This is your greatness, O well-born Maruts! — your
bounty extends far, as the sway of Aditi. Not even Indra
in his scorn can injure that bounty, on whatever man you
have bestowed it for his good deeds.

13. This is your kinship with us, O Maruts, that you,
immortals, in former years have often protected the singer.
Having through this prayer granted a hearing to man, all
these heroes together have become well known by their valiant
deeds.

14. That we may long flourish, O Maruts, with your
wealth, O ye racers, that our men may spread in the camp,
therefore let me achieve the rite with these offerings.

15. May this praise, O Maruts, this song of Mândârya,
the son of Mâna, the poet, ask you with food for offspring
for ourselves! May we have an invigorating autumn, with
quickening rain!

## BOOK I.— HYMN 167

### To the Maruts

1. O Indra, a thousand have been thy helps accorded to
us, a thousand, O driver of the bays, have been thy most

delightful viands. May thousands of treasures richly to
enjoy, may goods come to us a thousandfold.

2. May the Maruts come toward us with their aids, the
mighty ones, or with their best aids from the great heaven,
now that their furthest steeds have rushed forth on the distant shore of the sea;

3. There clings to the Maruts one who moves in secret,
like a man's wife (the lightning), and who is like a spear
carried behind, well grasped, resplendent, gold-adorned;
there is also with them Vac (the voice of thunder), like unto
a courtly, eloquent woman.

4. Far away the brilliant, untiring Maruts cling to their
young maid, as if she belonged to them all; but the terrible
ones did not drive away Rodasî (the lightning), for they
wished her to grow their friend.[11]

5. When the divine Rodasî with disheveled locks, the
manly minded, wished to follow them, she went, like Sûryâ
(the Dawn), to the chariot of her servant, with terrible look,
as with the pace of a cloud.

6. As soon as the poet with the libations, O Maruts, had
sung his song at the sacrifice, pouring out Soma, the youthful
men (the Maruts) placed the young maid in their chariot as
their companion for victory, mighty in assemblies.

7. I praise what is the praiseworthy true greatness of
those Maruts, that the manly minded, proud, and strong one
(Rodasî) drives with them toward the blessed mothers.

8. They protect Mitra and Varuna from the unspeakable,
and Aryaman also finds out the infamous. Even what is
firm and unshakable is being shaken; but he who dispenses
treasures, O Maruts, has grown in strength.

9. No people indeed, whether near to us, or from afar,
have ever found the end of your strength, O Maruts! The

[11] The spear of the Maruts is meant for the lightning. The rest of
this verse is difficult, and has been variously rendered by different
scholars. We must remember that the lightning is represented as the
wife or the beloved of the Maruts. In that character she is called
Rodasî, with the accent on the last syllable, and kept distinct from
*ródasî*, with the accent on the antepenultimate, which means " heaven
and earth."

Maruts, strong in daring strength, have, like the sea, boldly surrounded their haters.

10. May we to-day, may we to-morrow in battle be called the most beloved of Indra. We were so formerly, may we truly be so day by day, and may the lord of the Maruts be with us.

11. May this praise, O Maruts, this song of Mândârya, the son of Mâna, the poet, ask you with food for offspring for ourselves! May we have an invigorating autumn, with quickening rain!

## BOOK I.— HYMN 170

### Dialogue between Indra and his Worshiper, Agastya [12]

1. Indra: There is no such thing to-day, nor will it be so to-morrow. Who knows what strange thing this is? We must consult the thought of another, for even what we once knew seems to vanish.

2. Agastya: Why dost thou wish to kill us, O Indra? the Maruts are thy brothers; fare kindly with them, and do not strike us in battle.

3. The Maruts: O brother Agastya, why, being a

[12] The hymn admits of several explanations. There was a sacrifice in which Indra and the Maruts were invoked together, and it is quite possible that our hymn may owe its origin to this. But it is possible also that the sacrifice may be the embodiment of the same ideas which were originally expressed in this and similar hymns, namely, that Indra, however powerful by himself, could not dispense with the assistance of the storm-gods. The idea that a great god like Indra did not like to be praised together with others is an old idea, and we find traces of it in the hymns. It is quite possible, therefore, that our hymn contains the *libretto* of a little ceremonial drama in which different choruses of priests are introduced as preparing a sacrifice for the Maruts and for Indra, and as trying to appease the great Indra, who is supposed to feel slighted. Possibly Indra, and the Maruts, too, may have been actually represented by some actors, so that here, as elsewhere, the first seeds of the drama would be found in sacrificial performances. In the first verse Indra expresses his surprise in disconnected sentences, saying that such a thing has never happened before. The second line expresses that Indra does not remember such a thing, and must ask some one else, whether he remembers anything like it.

friend, dost thou despise us? We know quite well what thy mind was. Dost thou not wish to give to us?

4. AGASTYA: Let them prepare the altar; let them light the fire in front! Here we two will spread for thee the sacrifice, to be seen by the immortal.

5. AGASTYA: Thou rulest, O lord of treasures; thou, lord of friends, art the most generous. Indra, speak again with the Maruts, and then consume our offerings at the right season.

## BOOK V.— HYMN 61 [13]

### To the Maruts

1. Who are you, O men, the very best, who have approached one by one, from the farthest distance?

2. Where are your horses, where the bridles? How could you, how did you come? — the seat on the back, the rein in the nostrils?

3. Their goad is on the croup, the heroes stretched their legs apart. . . .

[13] This hymn is most unusual in the Rig-Veda in pausing for praise of a woman. The hymn is of a very composite nature. It is addressed to the Maruts by Syâvâsva. According to the commentaries, however, the Maruts are addressed in verses 1–4, 11–16 only; verses 5–8 are addressed to Sasîyasî Tarantamashishî, 9 to Purumîlha Vaidadasvi, 10 to Taranta Vaidadasvi, 17–19 to Rathavîti Dârbhya. The story told in the introductory verses is this: —" Arkanânas Atreya was chosen by Rathavîti Dârbhya to be his Ritvig priest. At the sacrifice Arkanânas saw the daughter of Rathavîti and asked her in marriage for his son Syâvâsva. Rathavîti consulted his wife, but she declined on the ground that no daughter of theirs had ever been given to a man who was not a poet (Rishi). Thereupon Syâvâsva performed penance, and traveled about collecting alms. He thus came to Sasîyasî, who recommended him, as a Rishi, to her husband, King Taranta. King Taranta was very generous to him, and sent him on to his younger brother, Purumîlha. On his way to Purumîlha, Syâvâsva saw the Maruts, and composed a hymn in their praise (verses 11–16). He had thus become a real poet or Rishi, and on returning home, he received from Rathavîti his daughter in marriage." Here therefore we have to deal with two princely brothers, both Vaidadasvis, namely Taranta and Purumîlha. They both give presents to Syâvâsva, who is a Brâhmana, and he marries the daughter of another prince, Rathavîti Dârbhya.

4. Move along, heroes, young men, the sons of an excellent mother, so that you may warm yourselves at our fire.[14]

5. May the woman, if she stretched out her arm as a rest for the hero, praised by *Syâvâsva*, gain cattle consisting of horses, cows, and a hundred sheep.

6. Many a woman is even more often kindlier than a godless and miserly man,

7. A woman who finds out the weak, the thirsty, the needy, and is mindful of the gods.

8. Even though many an unpraiseworthy miser (Pa*ni*) is called a man, she is worth as much in weregild.

9. Also the young woman joyfully whispered to me, to *Syâva*, the road — and the two bays went straight to Puru-milha, the wise, the far-famed,

10. Who gave me a hundred cows, like Vaidadasvi, like Taranta, in magnificence.

11. The Maruts, who drive on their quick horses, drinking the delightful mead, have gained glory here;

12. They on whose chariots Rodasî glitters in glory, like the golden disk above in heaven;

13. That youthful company of the Maruts, with blazing chariots, blameless, triumphant, irresistible.

14. Who now knows of them where the strikers rejoice, the well-born, the faultless?

15. You who are fond of praise, become the leaders of the mortal, listening to his imploring invocations; thus is my thought.

16. Bring then to us delightful and resplendent treasures, ye worshipful Maruts, destroyers of enemies.

17. O night, like a charioteer, carry away this hymn to Dârbhya, and these songs, O goddess.

18. And then tell him thus from me, "When Rathavîti offers Soma, my desire never goes away from me."

19. That mighty Rathavîti dwells among people rich in cattle, retired among the mountains.

---

[14] Evidently the sacrificial fire.

## BOOK VI.—HYMN 66

### To the Maruts

**1.** This may well be a marvel, even to an intelligent man, that anything should have taken the same name *dhenu,* cow: the one is always brimming to give milk among men, but Prisni (the cloud, the mother of the Maruts) poured out her bright udder once only.[15]

**2.** The Maruts who shone like kindled fires, as they grew stronger twice and thrice — their golden, dustless chariots became full of manly courage and strength.

**3.** They who are the sons of the bounteous Rudra, and whom she indeed was strong enough to bear; for she, the great, is known as the mother of the great, that very Prisni conceived the germ for the strong one (Rudra).

**4.** They who do not shrink from being born in this way, and who within the womb clean themselves from all impurity, when they have been brought forth brilliant, according to their pleasure, they sprinkle their bodies with splendor.

**5.** Among them there is no one who does not strive to be brought forth quickly; and they assume the defiant name of Maruts. They who are not unkind never tiring in strength, will the generous sacrificer be able to bring down these fierce ones?

**6.** Fierce in strength, followed by daring armies, these Maruts have brought together heaven and earth, both firmly established; then the self-shining Rodasî stood among the impetuous Maruts, like a light.

**7.** Even though your carriage, O Maruts, be without your deer, without horses, and not driven by any charioteer, without drag, and without reins, yet, crossing the air, it passes between heaven and earth, finishing its courses.

[15] The meaning seems to be that it is strange that two things, namely, a real cow and the cloud, *i.e.*, Prisni, the mother of the Maruts, should both be called *dhenu,* cow; that the one should always yield milk to men, while the other has her bright udder milked but once. This may mean that *dhenu,* a cow, yields her milk always, that *dhenu,* a cloud, yields rain but once, or, that Prisni gave birth but once to the Maruts.

8. No one can stop, no one can overcome him whom you, O Maruts, protect in battle. He whom you protect in his kith, his cattle, his kin, and his waters, he breaks the stronghold at the close of the day.

9. Offer a beautiful song to the host of the Maruts, the singers, the quick, the strong, who resist violence with violence; O Agni, the earth trembles before the champions.

10. Blazing like the flame of the sacrifices, flickering like the tongues of the fire, shouters, like roaring fighters, the flame-born Maruts are unassailable.

11. I invite with my call this strong and Marut-like son of Rudra, armed with flaming spears. Bright thoughts, like wild waters from the mountain, strove to reach the host of heaven.

## BOOK VII.— HYMN 56

### To the Maruts

1. Who are these resplendent men, dwelling together, the boys of Rudra, also with good horses?

2. No one indeed knows their births; they alone know each other's birthplace.

3. They plucked each other with their beaks; the hawks, rushing like the wind, strove together.

4. A wise man understands these secrets, that Prisni, the great, bore an udder.

5. May that clan be rich in heroes by the Maruts, always victorious, rich in manhood!

6. They are quickest to go, most splendid with splendor, endowed with beauty, strong with strength.

7. Strong is your strength, steadfast your powers, and thus by the Maruts is this clan mighty.

8. Resplendent is your breath, furious are the minds of the wild host, like a shouting maniac.

9. Keep from us entirely your flame; let not your hatred reach us here.

10. I call on the dear names of your swift ones, so that the greedy should be satisfied, O Maruts,

11. The well-armed, the swift, decked with beautiful chains, who themselves adorn their bodies.

12. Bright are the libations for you, the bright ones, O Maruts; a bright sacrifice I prepare for the bright. In proper order came those who truly follow the order, the bright born, the bright, the pure.

13. On your shoulders, O Maruts, are the rings, on your chests the golden chains are fastened; far-shining like lightnings with showers, you wield your weapons, according to your wont.

14. Your hidden splendors come forth; spread out your powers (names), O racers! Accept, O Maruts, this thousandfold, domestic share, as an offering for the house-gods.

15. If you thus listen, O Maruts, to this praise, at the invocation of the powerful sage, give him quickly a share of wealth in plentiful offspring, which no selfish enemy shall be able to hurt.

16. The Maruts, who are fleet like racers, the manly youths, shone like Yakshas; they are beautiful like boys standing round the hearth; they play about like calves who are still sucking.

17. May the bounteous Maruts be gracious to us, opening up to us the firm heaven and earth. May that bolt of yours, which kills cattle and men, be far from us! Incline to us, O Vasus, with your favors.

18. The Hotri priest calls on you again and again, sitting down and praising your common gift, O Maruts. O strong ones, he who is the guardian of so much wealth, he calls on you with praises, free from guile.

19. These Maruts stop the swift, they bend strength by strength, they ward off the curse of the plotter, and turn their heavy hatred on the enemy.

20. These Maruts stir up even the sluggard, even the vagrant, as the gods pleased. O strong ones, drive away the darkness, and grant us all our kith and kin.

21. May we not fall away from your bounty, O Maruts; may we not stay behind, O charioteers, in the distribution

of your gifts. Let us share in the brilliant wealth, the well-acquired, that belongs to you, O strong ones.

22. When valiant men fiercely fight together, for rivers, plants, and houses, then, O Maruts, sons of Rudra, be in battles our protectors from the enemy.

23. O Maruts, you have valued the praises which our fathers have formerly recited to you; with the Maruts the victor is terrible in battle, with the Maruts alone the racer wins the prize.

24. O Maruts, may we have a strong son, who is lord among men, a ruler, through whom we may cross the waters to dwell in safety, and then obtain our own home for you.

25. May Indra then, Varuna, Mitra, Agni, the waters, the plants, the trees of the forest be pleased with us. Let us be in the keeping, in the lap of the Maruts; protect us always with your favors.

## BOOK VII.— HYMN 59

### To the Maruts and Rudra

1. Whom you protect again and again, O gods, and whom you lead, to him, O Agni, Varuna, Mitra, Aryaman, and Maruts, yield your protection.

2. He who sacrifices, O gods, overcomes his enemies by your protection on a happy day. He who gives to your delight spreads forth his dwelling, spreads out much food.

3. This Vasishtha will not despise even the last among you, O Maruts; drink all of you, to-day, at my libation here, full of desire.

4. Your help does not indeed fail that man in battle to whom you granted it, O men! Your newest favor has turned hither; come quick then, ye who wish to drink.

5. O ye whose gifts are cheering, come to drink the juice of the Soma-flowers: these are your libations, O Maruts, for I gave them to you; do not go elsewhere!

6. Sit down on our altar and protect us, to give us bril-

liant riches. O Maruts, who never miss the Soma-mead, hail to you here to enjoy yourselves.

7. Having adorned their bodies, the swans with dark blue backs came flying in secret — the whole flock sat down all around me, like gay men, delighting in the Soma offering.

8. O Maruts, that hateful man who beyond our thoughts tries to hurt us, O Vasus, may he catch the snares of Druh; kill him with your hottest bolt!

9. O you Maruts, full of heat, here is the libation; be pleased to accept it, O you who destroy the enemies by your help.

10. O you who accept the domestic sacrifices, come hither, O Maruts; do not keep away, you who are bounteous by your help.

11. O Maruts, strong and wise, with sun-bright skins, I choose the sacrifice for you here and there.

12. We sacrifice to Tryambaka, the sweet-scented, wealth-increasing Rudra. May I be detached from death, like a gourd from its stem, but not from the immortal.

## BOOK II.— HYMN 33

### To Rudra, the Father of the Maruts

1. O father of the Maruts, let thy favor come near, and do not deprive us of the sight of the sun; may the hero Rudra be gracious to our horse, and may we increase in offspring, O Rudra!

2. May I attain to a hundred winters through the most blissful medicines which thou hast given! Put away far from us all hatred; put away anguish; put away sicknesses in all directions!

3. In beauty thou art the most beautiful of all that exists, O Rudra, the strongest of the strong, thou wielder of the thunderbolt! Carry us happily to the other shore of our anguish, and ward off all assaults of mischief.

4. Let us not incense thee, O Rudra, by our worship, not by bad praise, O hero, and not by divided praise! Raise up

our men by thy medicines, for I hear thou art the best of all physicians.

5. He who is invoked by invocations and libations, may I pay off that Rudra with my hymns of praise.  Let not him who is kind-hearted, who readily hears our call, the tawny, with beautiful cheeks, deliver us to this wrath!

6. The manly hero with the Maruts has gladdened me, the suppliant, with more vigorous health.  May I without mischief find shade, as if from sunshine; may I gain the favor of Rudra!

7. O Rudra, where is thy softly stroking hand which cures and relieves?  Thou, the remover of all heaven-sent mischief, wilt thou, O strong hero, bear with me?

8. I send forth a great, great hymn of praise to the bright tawny bull.  Let me reverence the fiery god with prostrations; we celebrate the flaring name of Rudra.

9. He, the fierce god, with strong limbs, assuming many forms, the tawny Rudra, decked himself with brilliant golden ornaments.  From Rudra, who is lord of this wide world, divine power will never depart.

10. Worthily thou bearest arrows and bow, worthily, O worshipful, the golden, variegated chain; worthily thou cuttest every fiend here to pieces, for there is nothing indeed stronger than thou, O Rudra.

11. Praise him, the famous, sitting in his chariot, the youthful, who is fierce and attacks like a terrible wild beast (the lion).  And when thou hast been praised, O Rudra, be gracious to him who magnifies thee, and let thy armies mow down others than us!

12. O Rudra, a boy indeed makes obeisance to his father who comes to greet him: I praise the lord of brave men, the giver of many gifts, and thou, when thou hast been praised, wilt give us thy medicines.

13. O Maruts, those pure medicines of yours, the most beneficent and delightful, O heroes, those which Manu, our father, chose — those I crave from Rudra, as health and wealth.

14. May the weapon of Rudra avoid us; may the great

anger of the flaring one pass us by. Unstring thy strong bows for the sake of our liberal lords, O bounteous Rudra; be gracious to our kith and kin.

15. Thus, O tawny and manly god, showing thyself, so as neither to be angry nor to kill, be mindful of our invocations, and, rich in brave sons, we shall magnify thee in the congregation.

## BOOK VI.—HYMN 74

### To Soma and Rudra

1. Soma and Rudra, may you maintain your divine dominion, and may the oblations reach you properly. Bringing the seven treasures to every house, be kind to our children and our cattle.

2. Soma and Rudra, draw far away in every direction the disease which has entered our house. Drive far away Nirriti, and may auspicious glories belong to us!

3. Soma and Rudra, bestow all these remedies on our bodies. Tear away and remove from us whatever evil we have committed, which clings to our bodies.

4. Soma and Rudra, wielding sharp weapons and sharp bolts, kind friends, be gracious unto us here! Deliver us from the snare of Varuna, and guard us, as kind-hearted gods!

## BOOK VII.—HYMN 46

### To Rudra

1. Offer ye these songs to Rudra whose bow is strong, whose arrows are swift, the self-dependent god, the unconquered conqueror, the intelligent, whose weapons are sharp — may he hear us!

2. For, being the lord, he looks after what is born on earth; being the universal ruler, he looks after what is born in heaven. Protecting us, come to our protecting doors, be without illness among our people, O Rudra!

3. May that thunderbolt of thine, which, sent from heaven, traverses the earth, pass us by! A thousand medicines are thine, O thou who art freely accessible; do not hurt us in our kith and kin!

4. Do not strike us, O Rudra; do not forsake us! May we not be in thy way when thou rushest forth furiously. Let us have our altar and a good report among men — protect us always with your favors!

## BOOK I.— HYMN 134

### To Vayu [16]

1. O Vayu, may the quick racers bring thee toward the offerings, to the early drink here, to the early drink of Soma! May Sûnrita (the Dawn) stand erect, approving thy mind! Come near on thy harnessed chariot to share, O Vayu, to share in the sacrifice!

2. May the delightful drops of Soma delight thee, the drops made by us, well-made, and heaven-directed, yes, made with milk, and heaven-directed. When his performed aids assume strength for achievement, our prayers implore the assembled steeds for gifts; yes, the prayers implore them.

3. Vayu yokes the two ruddy, Vayu yokes the two red horses, Vayu yokes to the chariot the two swift horses to draw in the yoke, the strongest to draw in the yoke. Awake Purandhi (the Morning) as a lover wakes a sleeping maid, reveal heaven and earth, brighten the dawn, yes, for glory brighten the dawn.

4. For thee the bright dawns spread out in the distance beautiful garments, in their houses, in their rays, beautiful in their new rays. To thee the juice-yielding cow pours out all treasures. Thou hast brought forth the Maruts from the flanks, yes, from the flanks of heaven.

5. For thee the white, bright, rushing Somas, strong in raptures, have rushed to the whirl, they have rushed to the whirl of the waters. The tired hunter asks luck of thee in

[16] Vayu is the wind; he is also in the next hymn addressed as Vata.

the chase; thou shieldest by thy power from every being,
yes, thou shieldest by thy power from powerful spirits.

6. Thou, O Vayu, art worthy as the first before all others
to drink these our Somas; thou art worthy to drink these
poured-out Somas. Among the people also who invoke thee
and have turned to thee, all the cows pour out the milk; they
pour out butter and milk for the Soma.

## BOOK X.— HYMN 168

### To Vâta

1. Now for the greatness of the chariot of Vâta! Its
roar goes crashing and thundering. It moves touching the
sky, and creating red sheens, or it goes scattering the dust
of the earth.

2. Afterward there rise the gusts of Vâta; they go toward
him, like women to a feast. The god goes with them on
the same chariot, he, the king of the whole of this world.

3. When he moves on his paths along the sky, he rests
not even a single day, the friend of the waters, the first-born,
the holy, where was he born, whence did he spring?

4. The breath of the gods, the germ of the world, that
god moves wherever he listeth; his roars indeed are heard,
not his form — let us offer sacrifice to that Vâta!

# HYMNS BY WOMEN

## BOOK I.— HYMN 179 [1]

1. LOPAMUDRA: Many years have I been serving thee diligently, both day and night, and through mornings, bringing on old age: decay now impairs the beauty of my limbs: what, therefore, is now to be done? Let husbands approach their wives.

2. The ancient sages, disseminators of truth, who, verily, conversed of truths with the gods, begot progeny, nor thereby violated their vow of continence; therefore should wives be approached by their husbands.

3. AGASTYA: Penance has not been practised in vain: since the gods protect us, we may indulge all our desires: in this world we may triumph in many conflicts, if we exert ourselves mutually together.

4. Desire, either from this cause or from that, has come upon me while engaged in prayer and suppressing passion: Let Lopamudra approach her husband: the unsteady female beguiles the firm and resolute man.

5. PUPIL: I beseech the Soma-juice, which has been drunk in my heart, that it may fully expiate the sin we have committed; man is subject to many desires.

6. Agastya, a venerable sage, working with prayer and sacrifice, desiring progeny, offspring, and strength, prac-

[1] This is one of the very few of the older poems of the Rig which seems to have but little of the character of a hymn. We must rather characterize it as a love-song or primeval drama. The princess Lopamudra sings the first two stanzas to her husband, the celebrated sage and ascetic Agastya. He answers in the next two stanzas. In the last two his pupils, or the chief among them, comment in the style of a Greek chorus. They regret their own sin in having listened curiously to the sage and his wife, but they approve Agastya's decision. This translation is by H. H. Wilson, Professor of Sanskrit at the University of Oxford.

tised both classes of obligations, and received true benedictions from the gods.

## BOOK X.— HYMN 125 [2]

1. I travel with the Rudras and the Vasus, with the Adityas and All-Gods I wander.
   I hold aloft both Varuna and Mitra, Indra, and Agni, and the pair of Asvins.

2. I cherish and sustain high-swelling Soma, and Tvashtar I support, Pushan and Bhaga.
   I load with wealth the zealous sacrificer who pours the juice and offers the oblation.

3. I am the Queen, the gatherer-up of treasures, most thoughtful, first of those who merit worship.
   Thus Gods have established me in many places with many homes to enter and abide in.

4. Through me alone all eat the food that feeds them — each man who sees, breathes, hears the word outspoken.
   They know it not, but yet they dwell beside me. Hear, one and all, the truth as I declare it.

5. I, verily, myself announce and utter the word that Gods and men alike shall welcome.
   I make the man I love exceedingly mighty, make him a sage, a Rishi, and a brahmin.

6. I bend the bow for Rudra that his arrow may strike and slay the hater of devotion.
   I rouse and order battle for the people, and I have penetrated earth and heaven.

7. On the world's summit I bring forth the Father: my home is in the waters, in the ocean.

[2] Tradition ascribes this hymn to the ascetic priestess, Vac. The word *Vac* also means " words," or " speech," or the " divine power of the spoken word." So that Vac is here both the authoress and the subject. The monotheistic spirit of the poem, its sense of a single all-embracing Power, and yet its feminine spirit of eager helpfulness, have made it much studied and admired. It has been often translated into English. The present accurate, yet musical, translation is by President R. T. Griffith of Benares College, India.

Thence I extend o'er all existing creatures, and touch even
yonder heaven with my forehead.

8. I breathe a strong breath like the wind and tempest, the
while I hold together all existence.

Beyond this wide earth and beyond the heavens I have
become so mighty in my grandeur.

## THE CREATION HYMN
### BOOK X.— HYMN 129 [3]

1. Then was not non-existent nor existent: there was no realm of air, no sky beyond it.
   What covered in, and where and what gave shelter? Was water there, unfathomed depth of water?

2. Death was not then, nor was there aught immortal: no sign was there, the day's and night's divider.
   That One Thing, breathless, breathed by its own nature: apart from it was nothing whatsoever.

3. Darkness there was: at first concealed in darkness this All was indiscriminated chaos.
   All that existed then was void and formless: by the great power of Warmth was born that Unit.

4. Thereafter rose Desire in the beginning — Desire, the primal seed and germ of Spirit.
   Sages who searched with their heart's thought discovered the existent's kinship in the non-existent.

5. Transversely was their severing line extended: what was above it then, and what below it?
   There were begetters, there were mighty forces, free action here and energy up yonder.

6. Who verily knows and who can here declare it, whence it was born and whence comes this creation?
   The Gods are later than this world's production. Who knows then whence it first came into being?

7. He, the first origin of this creation, whether he formed it all or did not form it,
   Whose eye controls this world in highest heaven, he verily knows it, or perhaps he knows not.

[3] This remarkable hymn is also given here in President Griffith's translation. Max Muller, in his "History of Ancient Sanskrit Literature," discusses it interestingly. It is certainly a most advanced and intellectual conception of creation, though some translators would turn it from the realm of science to that of theology by translating the "great power" of the third stanza not as "Warmth" but as deep "Contemplation."

## TO THE UNKNOWN GOD

### BOOK X.— HYMN 121 [4]

1. In the beginning there arose the Golden Child (Hiranya-garbha); as soon as born, he alone was the lord of all that is. He established the earth and this heaven: Who is the God to whom we shall offer sacrifice?

2. He who gives breath, he who gives strength, whose command all the bright gods revere, whose shadow is immortality, whose shadow is death: Who is the God to whom we shall offer sacrifice?

3. He who through his might became the sole king of the breathing and twinkling world, who governs all this, man and beast: Who is the God to whom we shall offer sacrifice?

4. He through whose might these snowy mountains are, and the sea, they say, with the distant river (the Rasa), he of whom these regions are indeed the two arms: Who is the God to whom we shall offer sacrifice?

5. He through whom the awful heaven and the earth were made fast, he through whom the ether was established, and the firmament; he who measured the air in the sky: Who is the God to whom we shall offer sacrifice?

---

[4] This translation is by Max Muller. The hymn is ascribed to Hiranya-garbha Prâgâpatya, and is supposed to be addressed to Ka, Who, *i.e.*, the Unknown God. This is one of the hymns which has always been suspected as modern by European interpreters. The reason is clear. To us the conception of one God, which pervades the whole of this hymn, seems later than the conception of many individual gods, as recognized in various aspects of nature, such as the gods of the sky, the sun, the storms, or the fire. And in a certain sense we may be right, and language also confirms our sentiment. In our hymn there are several words which do not occur again in the Rig-Veda, or which occur in places only which have likewise been suspected to be of more modern date. But when we say that a certain hymn is modern, we must carefully consider what we mean. Our hymn, for instance, must have existed previous to the Brâhmaṇa period, for many Brâhmaṇas presuppose it. Such a hymn can not be more "modern" than 1000 B. C.

6. He to whom heaven and earth, standing firm by his will, look up, trembling in their mind; he over whom the risen sun shines forth: Who is the God to whom we shall offer sacrifice?

7. When the great waters went everywhere, holding the germ (Hiranya-garbha), and generating light, then there arose from them the sole breath of the gods: Who is the God to whom we shall offer sacrifice?

8. He who by his might looked even over the waters which held power (the germ) and generated the sacrifice (light), he who alone is God above all gods: Who is the God to whom we shall offer sacrifice?

9. May he not hurt us, he who is the begetter of the earth, or he, the righteous, who begat the heaven; he who also begat the bright and mighty waters: Who is the God to whom we shall offer sacrifice?

10. Pragâpati, no other than thou embraces all these created things. May that be ours which we desire when sacrificing to thee: may we be lords of wealth![5]

[5] This last verse, identifying the "Unknown God" with Pragâpati, is generally regarded as a later addition.

# THE ATHARVA VEDA

### AND

# BRÂHMANAS

*" At the tip of my tongue honey, at the root of my tongue honeyedness; mayest thou be altogether in my power, mayest thou come unto my intent."*

—A CHARM OF THE ATHARVA VEDA.

# THE ATHARVA VEDA AND BRÂHMAÑAS

## (INTRODUCTION)

**T**HE Atharva Veda is so called because it is believed to have been preserved for centuries by the priests of the Atharvan race, before it was united with the other Vedas. Like the three older Vedas, it is divided into three portions: its original songs, which are called the Atharva Veda Samhita; the earlier commentaries on these called Brâhmañas, and the later commentaries. These commentaries are not necessarily of more recent date than those of the Rig-Veda; but in the song portion the Atharva Veda is not only written in a less ancient tongue than the Rig, but it has also a markedly different religious spirit. The songs of the Rig were joyous and self-confident; those of the Atharva are possessed with fear. They are mainly charms, defenses against evil spirits or other malign influences: In short, they are the voices of man's weakness and anxiety, not of his strength and courage. It has been suggested that this change may well be due to the Aryans having by this time conquered so much of India that they had absorbed much of the life and race of the conquered peoples, and something of their weakness. At all events the reading of the Atharvan hymns or charms in this section of our volume will impress upon the reader the darker tone of their religion.

Our scholars therefore are not inclined to reckon this Atharva Veda as being of older date than about 1000 B.C. This period would roughly coincide with that of the earliest Brâhmañas, or commentaries on the Vedic Songs. Some of these Brâhmañas therefore are also illustrated in the present section. The Brâhmañas, as already pointed out, are the prose explanations of the early priests, by which they not only sought to clarify the ancient songs, but gradually built around

53

them another faith — or at least a version of the old faith very different from its earlier visible form.

These Brâhmaas are full of legends, some quaint, some beautiful. The story of the flood has in it strange echoes of both the Babylonian story with its picture of the gods seeking man's worship, and of the Hebrew version with its depiction of sin as being the cause of the destruction of the race. Perhaps the Brâhmaas are not highly intellectual, since they deal more with folk-lore than philosophy; but we shall find in them the philosophic tendency which was later to produce the celebrated Upanishads.

# THE ATHARVA VEDA

## BOOK I.[1]—HYMN 1[2]

The thrice seven that go about, bearing all forms — let the lord of speech assign to me this day their powers, their selves.

Come again, lord of speech, together with divine mind; lord of good, make it stay; in me, in myself, be what is heard.

Just here stretch thou on, as it were the two tips of the bow with the bowstring; let the lord of speech make fast; in me, in myself, be what is heard.

Called on is the lord of speech; on us let the lord of speech call; may we be united with what is heard; let me not be parted with what is heard.

## BOOK I.—HYMN 34

### A Love-Spell: with a Sweet Herb[3]

This plant is honey-born; with honey we dig thee; forth from honey art thou engendered; so do thou make us possessed of honey.

[1] These hymns from the Atharva Veda are reprinted, by permission of Harvard University, from Volume Seven of the Harvard Oriental Series. They are the translations of Profs. Wm. D. Whitney and Charles R. Lanman.

[2] The hymn is called *trisaptiya*, from its second word; but it is further styled briefly *purva*, first, and generally quoted by that name. It is used in the ceremony for the "production of wisdom," and in those for the welfare of a Vedic student. It is further used, with various other passages, in the ceremony of entrance upon Vedic study; and it is also referred to, in an obscure way (probably as representing the whole Veda of which it is the beginning), in a number of other rites with which it has no apparent connection.

[3] This hymn is used in a ceremony for superiority in disputation: the ambitious disputant is to come into the assembly from the northeast,

At the tip of my tongue honey, at the root of my tongue honeyedness; mayest thou be altogether in my power, mayest thou come unto my intent.

Honeyed is my instepping, honeyed my forthgoing; with my voice I speak what is honeyed; may I be of honey-aspect.

Than honey am I sweeter, than the honey-plant more honeyed; of me verily shalt thou be fond, as of a honeyed branch.

About thee with an encompasing sugar-cane have I gone, in order to assure absence of mutual hatred; that thou mayest be one loving me, that thou mayest be one not going away from me.

## BOOK II.— HYMN 13

### For Welfare and Long Life of an Infant

Giving lifetime, O Agni, choosing old age; ghee-fronted, ghee-backed, O Agni — having drunk the sweet, pleasant ghee of the cow, do thou afterward defend this boy as a father his sons.

Envelop, put ye him for us with splendor; make ye him one to die of old age; make long life; Brihaspati furnished this garment unto King Soma for enveloping himself.

Thou hast put about thee this garment in order to well-being; thou hast become protector of the people against imprecation; both do thou live a hundred numerous autumns, and do thou gather about thee abundance of wealth.

Come, stand on the stone; let thy body become a stone; let all the gods make thy lifetime a hundred autumns.

Thee here, of whom we take the garment to be first worn, let all the gods favor; thee here, growing with good growth, let many brothers be born after, after thee, as one well born.

chewing the sweet plant. It is also used twice in the nuptial ceremonies, once with tying a *madugha* amulet on the finger, and once on crushing the amulet at the consummation of the marriage.

## BOOK II.—HYMN 15

### Against Fear

As both the heaven and the earth do not fear, are not harmed, so, my breath, fear not.

As both the day and night do not fear, are not harmed, so, my breath, fear not.

As both sacrament and dominion do not fear, are not harmed, so my breath, fear not.

As both truth and untruth do not fear, are not harmed, so, my breath, fear not.

As both what is and what is to be do not fear, are not harmed, so, my breath, fear not.

## BOOK II.—HYMN 17

### For Various Gifts

Force art thou; force mayest thou give me: hail!
Power art thou; power mayest thou give me: hail!
Strength art thou; strength mayest thou give me: hail!
Lifetime art thou; lifetime mayest thou give me: hail!
Hearing art thou; hearing mayest thou give me: hail!
Sight art thou; sight mayest thou give me: hail!
Protection art thou; protection mayest thou give me: hail!

## BOOK III.—HYMN 12

### Accompanying the Building of a House

Just here I fix my dwelling firm; may it stand in security, sprinkling ghee; unto thee here, O dwelling, may we resort with all our heroes, with good heroes, with unharmed heroes.

Just here stand thou firm, O dwelling, rich in horses, in kine, in pleasantness, in refreshment, in ghee, in milk; erect thyself in order to great good-fortune.

A garner art thou, O dwelling, of great roof, of cleansed grain; to thee may the calf come, may the boy, may the kine, streaming in at evening.

This dwelling let Savitar, Vayu, Indra, Brihaspati fix, foreknowing; let the Maruts sprinkle it with water, with ghee; let King Baga deepen our plowing.

O mistress of the building, as sheltering, pleasant, hast thou a goddess, been fixed by the gods in the beginning; clothing thyself in grass, mayest thou be well-willing; then mayest thou give us wealth together with heroes.

With due order, O beam, ascend the post; formidable, bearing rule, force away foes; let not the attendants of thy houses be harmed, O dwelling; may we live a hundred autumns with all our heroes.

To it the tender boy, to it the calf, with moving creatures, to it the jar of *parisrut,* with mugs of curd, have come.

Bring forward, O woman, this full jar, a stream of ghee combined with ambrosia; anoint these drinkers with ambrosia; let what is offered and bestowed defend it (the dwelling).

These waters I bring forward, free from *yaksma, yaksma*-effacing; I set forth unto the houses, along with immortal fire.

## BOOK III.— HYMN 15

### For Success in Trade

I stir up the trader, Indra; let him come to us, be our forerunner; thrusting away the niggard, the waylaying wild animal, let him, having the power, be giver of riches to me.

The many roads, traveled by the gods, that go about between heaven and earth — let them enjoy me with milk, with ghee, that dealing I may get riches.

With fuel, O Agni, with ghee, I, desiring, offer the oblation, in order to energize, to strengthen; revering with worship, so far as I am able — this divine prayer, in order to hundredfold winning.

This offense of ours mayest thou, O Agni, bear with, what

distant road we have gone. Successful for us be bargain and sale; let return-dealing make me fruitful; do ye two enjoy this oblation in concord; successful for us be our going about and rising.

With what riches I practise bargaining, seeking riches with riches, ye gods — let that become more for me, not less; O Agni, put down with the oblation the gain-slaying gods.

With what riches I practise bargaining, seeking riches with riches, ye gods — therein let Indra assign me pleasure, let Pragapati, Savitar, Soma, Agni.

Unto thee with homage do we, O priest Vaicvanara (for all men), give praise; do thou watch over our progeny, ourselves, our kine, our breaths.

Every day may we bring constantly for thee as for a standing horse, O Jatavedas; rejoicing together with abundance of wealth, with good, may we be thy neighbors, O Agni, take no harm.

## BOOK III.— HYMN 30

### For Concord

Like-heartedness, like-mindedness, non-hostility do I make for you; do ye show affection the one toward the other, as the inviolable cow toward her calf when born.

Be the son submissive to the father, like-minded with the mother; let the wife to the husband speak words full of honey, wealful.

Let not brother hate brother, nor sister sister; becoming accordant, of like courses, speak ye words auspiciously.

That incantation in virtue of which the gods do not go apart, nor hate one another mutually, we perform in your house, concord for your men.

Having superiors, intentful, be yet not divided, accomplishing together, moving on with joint labor; come hither speaking what is agreeable one to another; I make you united, like-minded.

Your drinking be the same, in common your share of food;

in the same harness do I join you together; worship ye Agni united, like spokes about a nave.

United, like-minded I make you, of one bunch, all of you, by my conciliation; be like the gods defending immortality; late and early be well-willing yours.

## BOOK IV.— HYMN 3

### Against Wild Beasts and Thieves

Up from here have stridden three — tiger, man, wolf; since, hey! go the rivers, hey! the divine forest-tree, hey! let the foes bow.

By a distant road let the wolf go, by a most distant also the thief; by a distant one the toothed rope, by a distant one let the malignant hasten.

Both thy two eyes and thy mouth, O tiger, we grind up; then all thy twenty claws.

The tigers, first of creatures with teeth, do we grind up; upon that also the thief; then the snake, the sorcerer; then the wolf.

What thief shall come to-day he shall go away smashed; let him go by the falling off of roads; let Indra smite him with the thunderbolt.

Ruined are the teeth of the beast; crushed in also are its ribs; disappearing be for thee the *godha;* downward go the lurking beast.

What thou contractest mayest thou not protract; mayest thou protract what thou dost not contract; Indra-born, Soma-born art thou, an Atharvan tiger-crusher.

# THE BRÂHMANAS

## THE CREATION OF NIGHT

### FROM THE MAITRAYANI BRÂHMANA [1]

Yama died.   The gods sought to console Yami for the loss of Yama.

When they asked her she said, " To-day hath he died."

They said, " In this way she will never forget him.   Night let us create."

Only day in those times existed — not night.   The gods created night.

Then came in existence the morrow.   Then she forgot him.

Therefore they say, " 'Tis days and nights make men forget sorrow."

## THE LEGEND OF THE FLOOD

### FROM THE CATA-PATHA BRÂHMANA

In the morning they brought to Manu water for washing, just as now also they are wont to bring water for washing the hands.   When he was washing himself, a fish came into his hands.

It spake to him the word, " Rear me, I will save thee! " " Wherefrom wilt thou save me? "   " A flood will carry away all these creatures: from that I will save thee! " " How am I to rear thee? "

It said, " As long as we are small, there is great destruction for us: fish devour fish.   Thou wilt first keep me in a jar.   When I outgrow that, thou wilt dig a pit and keep me

[1] From the " Sanskrit Reader," by Prof. Charles R. Lanman.

in it. When I outgrow that, thou wilt take me down to the sea, for then I shall be beyond destruction."

It soon became a *ghasha;* for that grows largest of all fish. Thereupon it said, "In such and such a year that flood will come. Thou shalt then attend to me (to my advice) by preparing a ship; and when the flood has risen thou shalt enter into the ship, and I will save thee from it."

After he had reared it in this way, he took it down to the sea, and in the same year which the fish had indicated to him, he attended to the advice of the fish by preparing a ship; and when the flood had risen, he entered into the ship. The fish then swam up to him, and to its horn he tied the rope of the ship, and by that means he passed swiftly up to yonder northern mountain.

It then said, "I have saved thee. Fasten the ship to a tree; but let not the water cut thee off whilst thou art on the mountain. As the water subsides, thou mayest gradually descend!" Accordingly he gradually descended, and hence the slope of the northern mountain is called "Manu's descent." The flood then swept away all these creatures, and Manu alone remained here.

Being desirous of offspring, he engaged in worshiping and austerities. During this time he also performed a *paka*-sacrifice: he offered up in the waters clarified butter, sour milk, whey, and curds. Thence a woman was produced in a year: becoming quite solid she rose; clarified butter gathered in her footprint. Mitra and Varuna met her.

They said to her, "Who art thou?" "Manu's daughter," she replied. "Say thou art ours," they said. "No," she said, "I am the daughter of him who begat me." They desired to have a share in her. She either agreed or did not agree, but passed by them. She came to Manu.

Manu said to her, "Who art thou?" "Thy daughter," she replied. "How, illustrious one, art thou my daughter?" he asked. She replied, "Those offerings of clarified butter, sour milk, whey, and curds, which thou madest in the waters, with them thou hast begotten me. I am the blessing (benediction): make use of me at the sacrifice! If thou wilt make use of me at the sacrifice, thou wilt become rich in offspring and cattle. Whatever blessing thou shalt invoke through me, all that shall be granted to thee!" He accordingly made use of her (as the benediction) in the middle of the sacrifice; for what is intermediate between the fore-offerings and the after-offerings is the middle of the sacrifice.

With her he went on worshiping and performing austerities, wishing for offspring. Through her he generated this race, which is this race of Manu; and whatever blessing he invoked through her, all that was granted to him.

Now this daughter of Manu is essentially the same as the Ida; [2] and whosoever, knowing this, performs with the Ida, he propagates this race which Manu generated; and whatever blessing he invokes through it (or her), all that is granted him.

## THE FOUNTAIN OF YOUTH

### From the Cata-patha Brâhmana

Now when the Bhrigus, or the Angiras, attained the heavenly world, Kyavana the Bhargava, or Kyavana the Angirasa, was left behind here on earth decrepit and ghostlike.

But Saryata, the Manava, just then wandered about here with his tribe, and settled near by that same place. His boys, while playing, setting that decrepit, ghostlike man at naught, pelted him with clods.

He was wroth with the Saryatas, and sowed discord among them: father fought with son, and brother with brother.

Saryata then bethought him —" This has come to pass for something or other I have done!" He caused the cowherds and shepherds to be called together, and said —

He said, " Which of you has seen anything here this day?" They said, " Yonder lies a man, decrepit and ghostlike: him

---

[2] Ida is the name given Manu's fish. It is also the word naming the collection of devotional ceremonies.

the boys have pelted with clods, setting him at naught."
Then Saryata knew that this was Kyavana.

He yoked his chariot, and putting his daughter Sukanya
thereon, he set forth, and came to the place where the Rishi
was.

He said, "Reverence be to thee, O Rishi; because I knew
thee not, therefore have I offended thee; here is Sukanya,
with her I make atonement to thee: let my tribe live at peace
together!" And from that same time his tribe lived at
peace together. But Saryata, the Manava, departed
forthwith, lest he should offend him a second time.

Now the Aswins [3] then wandered about here on earth performing cures. They came to Sukanya, and desired to win
her love; but she consented not thereto.

They said, "Sukanya, what a decrepit, ghostlike man is
that whom thou liest with; come and follow us!" She said,
"To whom my father has given me, him I will not abandon,
as long as he lives!" But the Rishi was aware of this.

He said, "Sukanya, what have those two said to thee?"
She told him all; and, when she had told him, he said, "If
they speak to thee thus again, say thou to them, 'But surely,
ye are neither quite complete nor quite perfect, and yet ye
deride my husband!' and if they say to thee, 'In what
respect are we incomplete, in what respect imperfect?' say
thou to them, 'Nay, make my husband young again, and I
will tell you!'" They came again to her and said to her
the same thing.

She said, "But surely ye are neither quite complete nor
quite perfect, and yet ye deride my husband!" They said,
"In what respect are we incomplete, in what respect imperfect?" She said, "Nay, make ye my husband young again,
and I will tell you!"

They said, "Take him down to yonder pool, and he shall
come forth with whatever age he shall desire!" She took
him down to that pool, and he came forth with the age he
desired.

They said, "Sukanya, in what respect are we incomplete,

[3] Aswins are lesser gods.

# THE UPANISHADS

"*From every sentence deep, original, and sublime thoughts arise, and the whole is pervaded by a high and holy and earnest spirit.*"

— SCHOPENHAUER.

"*In the whole world there is no study, except that of the originals, as beneficial and so elevating as that of the Oupnekhat [the first European translation of the Upanishads]. It has been the solace of my life; it will be the solace of my death.*"

— SCHOPENHAUER.

# THE UPANISHADS

## (INTRODUCTION)

THE Upanishads are to-day the most studied and the most admired portion of the Vedas. Each one of the four ancient Hymn Vedas has its supplementary "Brâhmana," consisting of early priestly commentary; and each of these has its supplement of later priestly commentary. These final productions, the most advanced and developed thought of all the Vedas, the most daring searches of the unknown achieved by the Hindu mind, these are called the Upanishads.

The name means "a sitting down under a master," or perhaps an entering into secret mysteries. The Upanishads, as the name implies, were long the most treasured teaching passed from mouth to mouth among the Brahmanic priesthood. Their total number seems to have approached two hundred, but not all of them have been discovered by European scholars. Perhaps some of them were never written down and are still kept secret by jealous masters. Judging from the language of the known Upanishads, they are of widely varying age; and our Western scholars have thought they could trace in them, as in the Hymn Vedas, the change and growth of Hindu thought. Certainly the Upanishads which are the most primitive in thought are also most ancient in style. So we give the reader here what is perhaps the oldest of the better-known ones, the Aitareya, with its solemn, half-mystic speculation on the creation and the three births of man.

After this we present some still more noted Upanishads, first the Mundaka. The Mundaka has at least this claim to age that it is written, like the old Hymn Vedas, in verse, instead of employing the usual Upanishad form of prose.

Moreover, the Mundaka serves as a sort of link between the public sacrifices or acts of worship conducted by means of the Hymn Vedas and the private acts of meditation represented by other Upanishads. Indeed, the Mundaka seems once to have been chanted in a public service. If so, it is a strangely deliberate setting aside of the older faith. It begins with kindly appraisal of the worth of what men had worshiped before, and then firmly dismisses this to assert that there is a higher life and knowledge.

Following this we give two brief but very celebrated Upanishads, so well known among the Hindus that they are usually called not by their true names but by their opening words. These are the Talavakara Upanishad, called the Kena, and the Vagasaneyi Upanishad, called the Isa. The Kena is the argument for the existence of Bráhmâ or of a Supreme God, and so calls itself the Brahmi-Upanishad. The Isa is the shortest and perhaps the deepest, sternest, and to our warmer life the most unhuman, of all the Indian Sacred Books. It tells how only by ignoring life can we rise above it.

Next, our volume gives the Upanishad most widely known to Europe and most noted for its lofty style and grandeur of idea, the Katha Upanishad. It has the form of a narrative in which Yama, the god of death, is persuaded to tell what man may learn through death, though even Yama warns the eager listener that he knows not the innermost truths of being. These lie beyond even death's wisdom.

Throughout the Upanishads there is frequent reference to the sacred syllable " Om," or perhaps it will be more clearly understood if spelt " Aum," since it consists of three Sanskrit sounds and so symbolizes the Brahman trinity. The true meaning of " Om " refers in some way to the concentration of the mind; that is to say, to "meditate on Om " means to make the mind blank to all outer impressions of the senses, to become solely and wholly an embodied thought. This intense concentration is demanded by all the Upanishads as being the first step toward any real knowledge and advance in spirit. The almost equally frequent word " Hari," when

used as an exclamation, signifies, " Peace ! "  Hence the
repeated formula of the brahmins, " Hari ! Om ! " might be
translated as " Let us meditate deeply and in peace. "  Or
when expressed, as it frequently is, as a prayer, it means,
" God give us peace and the wisdom won by meditation. "
This is the idea that pervades all the Upanishads.  Hari !
Om !

# THE UPANISHADS

## THE AITAREYA UPANISHAD

### FOURTH ADHYÂYA [1]

#### FIRST KHANDA

Adoration to the Highest Self. Hari, Om!

1. Verily, in the beginning [2] all this was Self, one only; there was nothing else blinking [3] whatsoever.

2. He thought: "Shall I send forth worlds?" He sent forth these worlds,

3. Ambhas (water), Mariki (light), Mara (mortal), and Ap (water).

4. That Ambhas (water) is above the heaven, and it is

---

[1] With this fourth adhyâya of an older Brâhmana begins the real Upanishad, best known under the name of the Aitareya Upanishad, and often separately edited, commented on, and translated. The difference between this Upanishad and earlier thought is easily perceived. Hitherto the answer to the question, Whence this world? had been, From Prana, prana meaning breath and life, which was looked upon for a time as a sufficient explanation of all that is. From a psychological point of view this prana is the conscious self (pragñâtman); in a more mythological form it appears as Hiranya-garbha, "the golden germ," sometimes even as Indra. It is one of the chief objects of the prânavidyâ, or life-knowledge, to show that the living principle in us is the same as the living principle in the sun, and that by a recognition of their identity and of the true nature of prana, the devotee, or he who has rightly meditated on prana during his life, enters after death into the world of Hiranya-garbha.

This, however, though it may have satisfied the mind of the Brahmans for a time, was not a final solution. That final solution of the problem not simply of life, but of existence, is given in this Upanishad which teaches that Atman, the Self, and not Prana, Life, is the last and only cause of everything. In some places this doctrine is laid down in all its simplicity. Our true self, it is said, has its true being in the Highest Self only. In other passages, however, and nearly in the whole of this Upanishad, this simple doctrine is mixed up with much that is mythological, fanciful, and absurd — arthavâda, as the commentators call it, but as it might often be more truly called, anarthavâda — and it is only toward the end that the identity of the self-conscious self with the Highest Self or Brahman is clearly enunciated.

[2] Before the creation.

[3] Blinking, *i.e.*, living.

72

## THE ETERNAL DANCE OF SHIVA.

*Shiva is the God of Life and Death. His dance is the movement of the universe and all who gaze upon this dance are held fascinated.*

heaven, the support. The Marîkis (the lights) are the sky. The Mara (mortal) is the earth, and the waters under the earth are the Ap world.[4]

5. He thought: " There are these worlds; shall I send forth guardians of the worlds? "

He then formed the Purusha (the person),[5] taking him forth from the water.[6]

6. He brooded on him, and when that person had thus been brooded on, a mouth burst forth like an egg. From the mouth proceeded speech, from speech Agni (fire).[7]

Nostrils burst forth. From the nostrils proceeded scent (prana), from scent Vayu (air).

Eyes burst forth. From the eyes proceeded sight, from sight Aditya (sun).

Ears burst forth. From the ears proceeded hearing, from hearing the Dis (quarters of the world).

Skin burst forth. From the skin proceeded hairs (sense of touch), from the hairs shrubs and trees.

The heart burst forth. From the heart proceeded mind, from mind Kandramas (moon).

The navel burst forth. From the navel proceeded the Apâna (the down-breathing),[8] from Apâna death.

[4] The names of the four worlds are peculiar. *Ambhas* means " water," and is the name given to the highest world, the waters above the heaven, and heaven itself. *Marîkis* are rays, here used as a name of the sky, *antariksha*. *Mara* means " dying," and the earth is called so, because all creatures living there must die. *Ap* is " water," here explained as the waters under the earth. The usual division of the world is three-fold: earth, sky, and heaven. Here it is fourfold, the fourth division being the water round the earth, or, as the commentator says, under the earth. *Ambhas* was probably intended for the highest heaven (*dyaus*), and was then explained both as what is above the heaven and as heaven itself, the support. If we translate, like Sankara and Colebrooke, " the water is the region above the heaven which heaven upholds," we should lose heaven altogether, yet heaven, as the third with sky and earth, is essential in the Indian view of the world.

[5] Purusha; " an embodied being " (Colebrooke); " a being of human shape " (Röer).

[6] According to the commentator, from the five elements, beginning with water.

[7] Three things are always distinguished here — the place of each sense, the instrument of the sense, and the presiding deity of the sense.

[8] The *Apâna,* down-breathing, is generally one of the five vital airs

The generative organ burst forth. From the organ proceeded seed, from seed water.

## Second Khanda

1. Those deities (devatâ), Agni and the rest, after they had been sent forth, fell into this great ocean.[9]

Then he (the Self) besieged him (the person) with hunger and thirst.

2. The deities then tormented by hunger and thirst spoke to him (the Self): "Allow us a place in which we may rest and eat food." [10]

He led a cow toward them (the deities). They said: "This is not enough." He led a horse toward them. They said: "This is not enough."

He led a man [11] toward them. Then they said: "Well done,[12] indeed." Therefore man is well done.

3. He said to them: "Enter, each according to his place."

4. Then Agni (fire), having become speech, entered the mouth. Vayu (air), having become scent, entered the nostrils. Aditya (sun), having become sight, entered the eyes. The Dis (regions), having become hearing, entered the ears. The shrubs and trees, having become hairs, entered the skin. Kandramas (the moon), having become mind, entered the heart. Death, having become down-breathing, entered the navel. The waters, having become seed, entered the generative organ.

5. Then Hunger and Thirst spoke to him (the Self): "Allow us two a place." He said to them: "I assign you to those very deities there; I make you co-partners with

which are supposed to keep the body alive. In our place, however, apâna is deglutition and digestion.

[9] They fell back into that universal being whence they had sprung, the first created person, the Virâg. Or they fell into the world, the last cause of which is ignorance.

[10] To eat food is explained to mean to perceive the objects which correspond to the senses, presided over by the various deities.

[11] Here purusha is different from the first purusha, the universal person. It can only be intended for intelligent man.

[12] Sukrita, well done, virtue; or, if taken for svakrita, self-made.

them." Therefore to whatever deity an oblation is offered, hunger and thirst are co-partners in it.

### THIRD KHANDA

1. He thought: "There are these worlds and the guardians of the worlds. Let me send forth food for them."

He brooded over the water.[13] From the water thus brooded on, matter [14] (*mûrti*) was born. And that matter which was born, that verily was food.[15]

2. When this food (the object-matter) had thus been sent forth, it wished to flee, crying and turning away. He (the subject) tried to grasp it by speech. He could not grasp it by speech. If he had grasped it by speech, man would be satisfied by naming food.

He tried to grasp it by scent (breath). He could not grasp it by scent. If he had grasped it by scent, man would be satisfied by smelling food.

He tried to grasp it by the eye. He could not grasp it by the eye. If he had grasped it by the eye, man would be satisfied by seeing food.

He tried to grasp it by the ear. He could not grasp it by the ear. If he had grasped it by the ear man would be satisfied by hearing food.

He tried to grasp it by the skin. He could not grasp it by the skin. If he had grasped it by the skin, man would be satisfied by touching food.

He tried to grasp it by the mind. He could not grasp it by the mind. If he had grasped it by the mind, man would be satisfied by thinking food.

He tried to grasp it by the generative organ. He could not grasp it by the organ. If he had grasped it by the organ, man would be satisfied by sending forth food.

He tried to grasp it by the down-breathing (the breath

13 The water, as mentioned before, or the five elements.

14 *Mûrti*, for *mûrtti*, "form" (Colebrooke); "a being of organized form," (Röer); *mûrtih, i.e.,* "vegetable food" for men, animal food for cats, etc.

15 Offered food, *i.e.,* objects for the Devatâs and the senses in the body.

which helps to swallow food through the mouth and to carry it off through the rectum, the pâyvindriya). He got it.

3. Thus it is Vayu (the getter) who lays hold of food, and the Vayu is verily Annâyu (he who gives life or who lives by food).

4. He thought: "How can all this be without me?"

5. And then he thought: "By what way shall I get there?" [16]

6. And then he thought: "If speech names, if scent smells, if the eye sees, if the ear hears, if the skin feels, if the mind thinks, if the off-breathing digests, if the organ sends forth, then what am I?"

7. Then opening the suture of the skull, he got in by that door.

8. That door is called the Vidriti (tearing asunder), the Nândana (the place of bliss).

9. There are three dwelling-places for him, three dreams; this dwelling-place (the eye), this dwelling-place (the throat), this dwelling-place (the heart).[17]

10. When born (when the Highest Self had entered the body) he looked through all things, in order to see whether anything wished to proclaim here another Self. He saw this person only (himself) as the widely spread Brahman. "I saw it," thus he said;

Therefore he was Idamdra (seeing this).

11. Being Idamdra by name, they call him Indra mysteriously. For the Devas love mystery, yea, they love mystery.

[16] Or, by which of the two ways shall I get in, the one way being from the top of the foot, the other from the skull?

[17] Passages like this must always have required an oral interpretation, but it is by no means certain that the explanation given in the commentaries represents really the old traditional interpretation. Sâyana explains the three dwelling-places as the right eye, in a state of waking; as the throat, in a state of dreaming; as the heart, in a state of profound sleep. Sankara explains them as the right eye, the inner mind, and the ether in the heart. Sâyana allows another interpretation of the three dwelling-places being the body of the father, the body of the mother, and one's own body. The three dreams or sleeps he explains by waking, dreaming, and profound sleep, and he remarks that waking, too, is called a dream as compared with the true awakening, which is the knowledge of Brahman. In the last sen-

### FIFTH ADHYÂYA

#### FIRST KHANDA

1. Let the women who are with child move away!

2. Verily, from the beginning he (the Self) is in man as a germ, which is called seed.

3. This seed, which is strength gathered from all the limbs of the body, he (the man) bears as self in his self (body). When he commits the seed to the woman, then he (the father) causes it to be born. That is his first birth.

4. That seed becomes the self of the woman, as if one of her own limbs. Therefore it does not injure her.

5. She nourishes his (her husband's) self (the son) within her. She who nourishes is to be nourished.

6. The woman bears the germ. He (the father) elevates the child even before the birth, and immediately after.[18]

7. When he thus elevates the child both before and after his birth, he really elevates his own self,

8. For the continuation of these worlds (men). For thus are these worlds continued.

9. This is his second birth.

10. He (the son), being his self, is then placed in his stead for the performance of all good works.

11. But his other self (the father), having done all he has to do, and having reached the full measure of his life, departs.

12. And departing from hence he is born again. That is his third birth.

13. And this has been declared by a Rishi.

14. "While dwelling in the womb, I discovered all the births of these Devas. A hundred iron strongholds kept me, but I escaped quickly down like a falcon."

15. Vâmadeva, lying in the womb, has thus declared this.

And having this knowledge he stepped forth, after this dissolution of the body, and having obtained all his desires

tence the speaker, when repeating three times " this dwelling-place," is supposed to point to his right eye, the throat, and the heart.

[18] By nourishing the mother, and by performing certain ceremonies both before and after the birth of a child.

in that heavenly world, became immortal, yea, he became immortal.

## SIXTH ADHYÂYA

### First Khanda

1. Let the women go back to their place.

2. Who is he whom we meditate on as the Self? Which is the Self?

3. That by which we see form, that by which we hear sound, that by which we perceive smells, that by which we utter speech, that by which we distinguish sweet and not sweet, and what comes from the heart and the mind, namely, perception, command, understanding, knowledge, wisdom, seeing, holding, thinking, considering, readiness (or suffering), remembering, conceiving, willing, breathing, loving, desiring?

4. No, all these are various names only of knowledge (the true Self).

5. And that Self, consisting of knowledge, is Brahman, it is Indra, it is Pragâpati. All these Devas, these five great elements, earth, air, ether, water, fire — these and those which are, as it were, small and mixed, and seeds of this kind and that kind, born from eggs, born from the womb, born from heat, born from germs, horses, cows, men, elephants, and whatsoever breathes, whether walking or flying, and what is immovable — all that is led (produced) by knowledge (the Self).

6. It rests on knowledge (the Self). The world is led (produced) by knowledge (the Self). Knowledge is its cause.[19]

7. Knowledge is Brahman.

8. He (Vâmadeva), having by this conscious self stepped forth from this world, and having obtained all desires in

---

[19] We have no words to distinguish between *pragñâ,* "state of knowing," and *pragñâna,* "act of knowing." Both are names of the Highest Brahman, which is the beginning and end (*pratishthâ*) of everything that exists or seems to exist.

that heavenly world, became immortal, yea, he became immortal. Thus it is, Om.

### SEVENTH ADHYÂYA [20]

#### FIRST KHANDA

1. My speech rests in the mind, my mind rests in speech.[21] Appear to me, thou, the Highest Self! You (speech and mind) are the two pins that hold the wheels of the Veda. May what I have learnt not forsake me. I join day and night with what I have learnt.[22] I shall speak of the real, I shall speak the true. May this protect me; may this protect the teacher! May it protect me; may it protect the teacher, yea, the teacher!

[20] This seventh adhyâya contains a propitiatory prayer. It is frequently left out in the MSS. which contain the Aitareya Upanishad with Sankara's commentary.

[21] The two depend on each other.

[22] I repeat it day and night so that I may not forget it.

## THE MUNDAKA UPANISHAD

### FIRST MUNDAKA

#### First Khanda

1. Bráhmâ was the first of the Devas, the maker of the universe, the preserver of the world. He told the knowledge of Brahman, the foundation of all knowledge, to his eldest son Atharvan.

2. Whatever Bráhmâ told Atharvan, that knowledge of Brahman Atharvan formerly told to Angir; he told it to Satyavâha Bhâradvâga, and Bhâradvâga, told it in succession to Angiras.

3. Saunaka, the great householder, approached Angiras respectfully and asked: " Sir, what is that through which, if it is known, everything else becomes known ? "

4. He said to him: " Two kinds of knowledge must be known, this is what all who know Brahman tell us, the higher and the lower knowledge.

5. " The lower knowledge is the Rig-Veda, Yagur-Veda, Sâma-Veda, Atharva-Veda, Sikshâ (phonetics), Kalpa (ceremonial), Vyâkarana (grammar), Nirukta (etymology), Khandas (meter), Gyotisha (astronomy); but the higher knowledge is that by which the Indestructible (Brahman) is apprehended.

6. " That which can not be seen, nor seized, which has no family and no caste, no eyes nor ears, no hands nor feet, the eternal, the omnipresent (all-pervading), infinitesimal, that which is imperishable, that it is which the wise regard as the source of all beings.

7. " As the spider sends forth and draws in its thread, as plants grow on the earth, as from every man hairs spring forth on the head and the body, thus does everything arise here from the Indestructible.

8. " The Brahman swells by means of brooding (pen-

ance) [1]; hence is produced matter (food); from matter breath, mind, the true, the worlds (seven), and from the works performed by men in the worlds, the immortal (the eternal effects, rewards, and punishments of works).

9. " From him who perceives all and who knows all, whose brooding (penance) consists of knowledge from him (the highest Brahman) is born that Brahman, name, form, and matter (food)."

## SECOND KHANDA

1. This is the truth;[2] the sacrificial works which they (the poets) saw in the hymns of the Veda have been performed in many ways in the Tretâ age.[3]  Practise them diligently, ye lovers of truth, this is your path that leads to the world of good works!

2. When the fire is lighted and the flame flickers, let a man offer his oblations between the two portions of melted butter, as an offering with faith.

3. If a man's Agnihotra sacrifice [4] is not followed by the new-moon and full-moon sacrifices, by the four-months' sacrifices, and by the harvest sacrifice, if it is unattended by guests, not offered at all, or without the Vaisvadeva ceremony, or not offered according to rule, then it destroys his seven worlds.[5]

[1] I have translated *tapas* by "brooding," because this is the only word in English which combines the two meanings of warmth and thought.  Native authorities actually admit two roots, one "to burn," the other "to meditate."

[2] In the beginning of the second khanda the lower knowledge is first described, referring to the performance of sacrifices and other good deeds. The reward of them is perishable, and therefore a desire is awakened after the higher knowledge.

[3] The Tretâ age is frequently mentioned as the age of sacrifices.

[4] The Agnihotra is the first of all sacrifices, and the type of many others.  Oblations to the gods are to be offered.  There are two oblations in the morning to Sûrya and Pragâpati, two in the evening to Agni and Pragâpati.  Other sacrifices, such as those mentioned in verse 3, are connected with the Agnihotra.

[5] The seven worlds form the rewards of a pious sacrificer, the first is Bhuh, the last Satya.  The seven worlds may also be explained as the worlds of the father, grandfather, and great-grandfather, of the son, the grandson, and great-grandson, and of the sacrificer himself.

4. Kâlî (black), Karâlî (terrific), Manogavâ (swift as thought), Sulohitâ (very red), Sudhûmravarnâ (purple), Sphulinginî (sparkling), and the brilliant Visvarûpî (having all forms), all these playing about are called the seven tongues of fire.

5. If a man performs his sacred works when these flames are shining, and the oblations follow at the right time, then they lead him as sun-rays to where the one Lord of the Devas dwells.

6. Come hither, come hither! the brilliant oblations say to him, and carry the sacrificer on the rays of the sun, while they utter pleasant speech and praise him, saying: "This is thy holy Brâhmâ-world (Svarga), gained by thy good works."

7. But frail, in truth, are those boats, the sacrifices, the eighteen, in which this lower ceremonial has been told. Fools who praise this as the highest good, are subject again and again to old age and death.

8. Fools dwelling in darkness, wise in their own conceit, and puffed up with vain knowledge, go round and round staggering to and fro, like blind men led by the blind.

9. Children, when they have long lived in ignorance, consider themselves happy. Because those who depend on their good works are, owing to their passions, improvident, they fall and become miserable when their life in the world which they had gained by their good works is finished.

10. Considering sacrifice and good works as the best, these fools know no higher good, and having enjoyed their reward on the height of heaven, gained by good works, they enter again this world or a lower one.

11. But those who practise penance and faith in the forest, tranquil, wise, and living on alms, depart free from passion through the sun to where that immortal Person dwells whose nature is imperishable.

12. Let a Brâhmana, after he has examined all these worlds which are gained by works, acquire freedom from all desires. Nothing that is eternal (not made) can be gained by what is not eternal (made). Let him, in order to under-

stand this, take fuel in his hand and approach a Guru who is learned and dwells entirely in Brahman.

13. To that pupil who has approached him respectfully, whose thoughts are not troubled by any desires, and who has obtained perfect peace, the wise teacher truly told that knowledge of Brahman through which he knows the eternal and true Person.

## SECOND MUNDAKA

### FIRST KHANDA

1. This is the truth. As from a blazing fire sparks, being like unto fire, fly forth a thousandfold, thus are various beings brought forth from the Imperishable, my friend, and return thither also.

2. That heavenly Person is without body, he is both without and within, not produced, without breath and without mind, pure, higher than the high Imperishable.

3. From him when entering on creation are born breath, mind, and all organs of sense, ether, air, light, water, and the earth, the support of all.

4. Fire (the sky) is his head, his eyes the sun and the moon, the quarters his ears, his speech the Vedas disclosed, the wind his breath, his heart the universe; from his feet came the earth; he is indeed the inner Self of all things.

5. From him comes Agni (fire), the sun being the fuel; from the moon (Soma) comes rain (Parganya); from the earth herbs; and man gives seed unto the woman. Thus many beings are begotten from the Person (purusha).

6. From him come the Rig, the Sâman, the Yagush, the Dîkshâ (initiatory rites), all sacrifices and offerings of animals, and the fees bestowed on priests, the year too, the sacrificer, and the worlds, in which the moon shines brightly and the sun.

7. From him the many Devas too are begotten, the Sâdhyas (genii), men, cattle, birds, the up and down breathings, rice and corn for sacrifices, penance, faith, truth, abstinence, and law.

8. The seven senses (prana) also spring from him, the seven lights (acts of sensation), the seven kinds of fuel (objects by which the senses are lighted), the seven sacrifices (results of sensation), these seven worlds (the places of the senses, the worlds determined by the senses) in which the senses move, which rest in the cave of the heart, and are placed there seven and seven.

9. Hence come the seas and all the mountains, from him flow the rivers of every kind; hence come all herbs and the juice through which the inner Self subsists with the elements.

10. The Person is all this, sacrifice, penance, Brahman, the highest immortal; he who knows this hidden in the cave of the heart, he, O friend, scatters the knot of ignorance here on earth.

## Second Khanda

1. Manifest, near, moving in the cave of the heart is the great Being. In it everything is centered which ye know as moving, breathing, and blinking, as being and not-being, as adorable, as the best, that is beyond the understanding of creatures.

2. That which is brilliant, smaller than small, that on which the worlds are founded and their inhabitants, that is the indestructible Brahman, that is the breath, speech, mind; that is the true, that is the immortal. That is to be hit. Hit it, O friend!

3. Having taken the Upanishad as the bow, as the great weapon, let him place on it the arrow, sharpened by devotion! Then having drawn it with a thought directed to that which is, hit the mark, O friend, viz., that which is the Indestructible!

4. Om is the bow, the Self is the arrow, Brahman is called its aim. It is to be hit by a man who is not thoughtless; and then, as the arrow becomes one with the target, he will become one with Brahman.

5. In him the heaven, the earth, and the sky are woven, the mind also with all the senses. Know him alone as the

Self, and leave off other words! He is the bridge of the Immortal.

6. He moves about becoming manifold within the heart where the arteries meet, like spokes fastened to the nave. Meditate on the Self as Om! Hail to you that you may cross beyond the sea of darkness!

7. He who understands all and who knows all, he to whom all this glory in the world belongs, the Self, is placed in the ether, in the heavenly city of Brahman (the heart). He assumes the nature of mind, and becomes the guide of the body of the senses. He subsists in food, in close proximity to the heart. The wise who understand this, behold the Immortal which shines forth full of bliss.

8. The fetter of the heart is broken, all doubts are solved, all his works and their effects perish when he has been beheld who is high and low (cause and effect).

9. In the highest golden sheath there is the Brahman without passions and without parts. That is pure, that is the light of lights, that is it which they know who knows the Self.

10. The sun does not shine there, nor the moon and the stars, nor these lightnings, and much less this fire. When he shines, everything shines after him; by his light all this is lighted.

11. That immortal Brahman is before, that Brahman is behind, that Brahman is right and left. It has gone forth below and above; Brahman alone is all this; it is the best.


### THIRD MUNDAKA

#### First Khanda

1. Two birds, inseparable friends, cling to the same tree. One of them eats the sweet fruit, the other looks on without eating.

2. On the same tree man sits grieving, immersed, bewildered by his own impotence (an-îsa). But when he sees the

other lord (îsa) contented and knows his glory, then his grief passes away.

3. When the seer sees the brilliant maker and lord of the world as the Person who has his source in Brahman, then he is wise, and shaking off good and evil, he reaches the highest oneness, free from passions;

4. For he is the Breath shining forth in all beings, and he who understands this becomes truly wise, not a talker only. He revels in the Self, he delights in the Self, and having performed his works (truthfulness, penance, meditation, etc.) he rests, firmly established in Brahman, the best of those who know Brahman.

5. By truthfulness, indeed, by penance, right knowledge, and abstinence must that Self be gained; the Self whom spotless anchorites gain is pure, and like a light within the body.

6. The true prevails, not the untrue; by the true the path is laid out, the way of the gods (devayânah), on which the old sages, satisfied in their desires, proceed to where there is that highest place of the True One.

7. That (true Brahman) shines forth grand, divine, inconceivable, smaller than small; it is far beyond what is far and yet near here, it is hidden in the cave of the heart among those who see it even here.

8. He is not apprehended by the eye, nor by speech, nor by the other senses, not by penance or good works. When a man's nature has become purified by the serene light of knowledge, then he sees him, meditating on him as without parts.

9. That subtle Self is to be known by thought (ketas) there where breath has entered fivefold; for every thought of men is interwoven with the senses, and when thought is purified, then the Self arises.

10. Whatever state a man whose nature is purified imagines, and whatever desires he desires for himself or for others, that state he conquers and those desires he obtains. Therefore let every man who desires happiness worship the man who knows the Self.

## SECOND KHANDA

1. He (the knower of the Self) knows that highest home of Brahman, in which all is contained and shines brightly. The wise who, without desiring happiness, worship that Person, transcend this seed; they are not born again.

2. He who forms desires in his mind is born again through his desires here and there. But to him whose desires are fulfilled, and who is conscious of the true Self within himself, all desires vanish, even here on earth.

3. That Self can not be gained by the Veda, nor by understanding, nor by much learning. He whom the Self chooses, by him the Self can be gained. The Self chooses him (his body) as his own.

4. Nor is that Self to be gained by one who is destitute of strength, or without earnestness, or without right meditation. But if a wise man strives after it by those means (by strength, earnestness, and right meditation), then his Self enters the home of Brahman.

5. When they have reached him (the Self), the sages become satisfied through knowledge, they are conscious of their Self, their passions have passed away, and they are tranquil. The wise, having reached him who is omnipresent everywhere, devoted to the Self, enter into him wholly.

6. Having well ascertained the object of the knowledge of the Vedanta, and having purified their nature by the Yoga of renunciation, all anchorites, enjoying the highest immortality, become free at the time of the great end (death) in the worlds of Bráhmá.

7. Their fifteen parts enter into their elements, their Devas (the senses) into their corresponding Devas. Their deeds and their Self with all his knowledge become all one in the highest Imperishable.

8. As the flowing rivers disappear in the sea, losing their name and their form, thus a wise man, freed from name and form, goes to the divine Person, who is greater than the great.

9. He who knows that highest Brahman becomes even Brahman. In his race no one is born ignorant of Brahman.

He overcomes grief, he overcomes evil; free from the fetters of the heart, he becomes immortal.

10. And this is declared by the following Rig-verse: "Let a man tell this science of Brahman to those only who have performed all necessary acts, who are versed in the Vedas, and firmly established in the lower Brahman, who themselves offer an oblation the one Rishi (Agni), full of faith, and by whom the rite of carrying fire on the head has been performed, according to the rule of the Atharvanas."

11. The Rishi Angiras formerly told this true science; a man who has not performed the proper rites does not read it. Adoration to the highest Rishis! Adoration to the highest Rishis!

## THE KENA UPANISHAD

### First Khanda

1. The Pupil asks: "At whose wish does the mind sent forth proceed on its errand? At whose command does the first breath go forth? At whose wish do we utter this speech? What god directs the eye, or the ear?"

2. The Teacher replies: "It is the ear of the ear, the mind of the mind, the speech of speech, the breath of breath, and the eye of the eye. When freed from the senses the wise, on departing from this world, become immortal.[1]

3. "The eye does not go thither, nor speech, nor mind. We do not know, we do not understand, how any one can teach it.

4. "It is different from the known, it is also above the unknown, thus we have heard from those of old, who taught us this.

5. "That which is not expressed by speech and by which speech is expressed, that alone know as Brahman, not that which people here adore.

6. "That which does not think by mind, and by which, they say, mind is thought, that alone know as Brahman, not that which people here adore.

7. "That which does not see by the eye, and by which one sees the work of the eyes, that alone know as Brahman, not that which people here adore.

8. "That which does not hear by the ear, and by which the ear is heard, that alone know as Brahman, not that which people here adore.

[1] This verse admits of various translations, and still more various explanations. What is meant by the ear of the ear is very fully explained by the commentator, but the simplest acceptation would seem to take it as an answer to the preceding questions, so that the ear of the ear should be taken for him who directs the ear, *i.e.*, the Self, or Brahman. This will become clearer as we proceed.

9. "That which does not breathe by breath, and by which breath is drawn, that alone know as Brahman, not that which people here adore."

### SECOND KHANDA

1. The Teacher says: "If thou thinkest I know it well, then thou knowest surely but little, what is that form of Brahman known, it may be, to thee?"

2. The Pupil says: "I do not think I know it well, nor do I know that I do not know it. He among us who knows this, he knows it, nor does he know that he does not know it.[2]

3. "He by whom it (Brahman) is not thought, by him it is thought; he by whom it is thought, knows it not. It is not understood by those who understand it, it is understood by those who do not understand it.

4. "It is thought to be known as if by awakening, and then we obtain immortality indeed. By the Self we obtain strength, by knowledge we obtain immortality.

5. "If a man know this here, that is the true end of life; if he does not know this here, then there is great destruction (new births). The wise who have thought on all things and recognized the Self in them become immortal, when they have departed from this world."

### THIRD KHANDA [3]

1. Brahman obtained the victory for the Devas. The Devas became elated by the victory of Brahman, and they

---

[2] This verse has again been variously explained. Apparently the train of thought is this: We can not know Brahman, as we know other objects, by referring them to a class and pointing out their differences. But, on the other hand, we do not know that we know him not, i.e., no one can assert that we know him not, for we want Brahman in order to know anything. He, therefore, who knows this double peculiarity of the knowledge of Brahman, he knows Brahman, as much as it can be known; and he does not know, nor can anybody prove it to him, that he does not know Brahman.

[3] This khanda is generally represented as a later addition, but its prose style has more of a Brâhmaṇa character than the verses in the preceding khandas, although their metrical structure is irregular, and may be taken as a sign of antiquity.

thought, this victory is ours only, this greatness is ours only.

2. Brahman perceived this and appeared to them. But they did not know it, and said: "What sprite (yaksha or yakshya) is this?"

3. They said to Agni (fire): "O Gâtavedas, find out what sprite this is." "Yes," he said.

4. He ran toward it, and Brahman said to him: "Who are you?" He replied: "I am Agni, I am Gâtavedas."

5. Brahman said: "What power is in you?" Agni replied: "I could burn all whatever there is on earth."

6. Brahman put a straw before him, saying: "Burn this." He went toward it with all his might, but he could not burn it. Then he returned thence and said: "I could not find out what sprite this is."

7. Then they said to Vayu (air): "O Vayu, find out what sprite this is." "Yes," he said.

8. He ran toward it, and Brahman said to him: "Who are you?" He replied: "I am Vayu, I am Mâtarisvan."

9. Brahman said: "What power is in you?" Vayu replied: "I could take up all whatever there is on earth."

10. Brahman put a straw before him, saying: "Take it up." He went toward it with all his might, but he could not take it up. Then he returned thence and said: "I could not find out what sprite this is."

11. Then they said to Indra: "O Maghavan, find out what sprite this is." He went toward it, but it disappeared from before him.

12. Then in the same space (ether) he came toward a woman, highly adorned: it was Umâ, the daughter of Himavat.[4] He said to her: "Who is that sprite?"

---

[4] Umâ may here be taken as the wife of Śiva, daughter of Himavat, better known by her earlier name, Pârvatî, the daughter of the mountains. Originally she was, not the daughter of the mountains or of the Himalaya, but the daughter of the cloud, just as Rudra was originally, not the lord of the mountains, *girîsa*, but the lord of the clouds. We are, however, moving here in a secondary period of Indian thought, in which we see, as among Semitic nations, the manifested powers, and particularly the knowledge and wisdom of the gods, represented by their wives.

## Fourth Khanda

1. She replied: "It is Brahman. It is through the victory of Brahman that you have thus become great." After that he knew that it was Brahman.

2. Therefore these Devas, *viz.*, Agni, Vayu, and Indra, are, as it were, above the other gods, for they touched it (the Brahman) nearest.

3. And therefore Indra is, as it were, above the other gods, for he touched it nearest, he first knew it.

4. This is the teaching of Brahman, with regard to the gods (mythological): It is that which now flashes forth in the lightning, and now vanishes again.

5. And this is the teaching of Brahman, with regard to the body (psychological): It is that which seems to move as mind, and by it imagination remembers again and again.[5]

6. That Brahman is called Tadvana,[6] by the name of Tadvana it is to be meditated on. All beings have a desire for him who knows this.

7. The Teacher: "As you have asked me to tell you the

[5] I have translated these paragraphs very differently from Sankara and other interpreters. The wording is extremely brief, and we can only guess the original intention of the Upanishad by a reference to other passages. Now the first teaching of Brahman, by means of a comparison with the gods or heavenly things in general, seems to be that Brahman is what shines forth suddenly like lightning. Sometimes the relation between the phenomenal world and Brahman is illustrated by the relation between bubbles and the sea, or lightning and the unseen heavenly light. In another passage lightning, when no longer seen, is to facilitate the conception of the reality of things, as distinct from their perceptibility. I think, therefore, that the first simile, taken from the phenomenal world, was meant to show that Brahman is that which appears for a moment in the lightning, and then vanishes from our sight.

The next illustration is purely psychological. Brahman is proved to exist, because our mind moves toward things, because there is something in us which moves and perceives, and because there is something in us which holds our perceptions together (*sankalpa*), and revives them again by memory.

I give my translation as hypothetical only, for certainty is extremely difficult to attain, when we have to deal with these enigmatical sayings which, when they were first delivered, were necessarily accompanied by oral explanations.

[6] Tadvana, as a name of Brahman, is explained as "the desire of it."

## UMA WINS HER GOD LOVER.

*By suppressing every human passion, Uma becomes the wife
of Shiva, God of Life and Death.*

Upanishad, the Upanishad has now been told you.   We have told you the Brâhmî Upanishad.

8. " The feet on which that Upanishad stands are penance, restraint, sacrifice; the Vedas are all its limbs, the True is its abode.

9. " He who knows this Upanishad, and has shaken off all evil, stands in the endless, unconquerable world of heaven, yea, in the world of heaven."

## THE ISA UPANISHAD

1. All this, whatsoever moves on earth, is to be hidden in the Lord (the Self). When thou hast surrendered all this, then thou mayest enjoy. Do not covet the wealth of any man!

2. Though a man may wish to live a hundred years, performing works, it will be thus with him; but not in any other way: work will thus not cling to a man.

3. There are the worlds of the Asuras covered with blind darkness. Those who have destroyed their Self, who perform works, without having arrived at a knowledge of the true Self, go after death to those worlds.

4. That one (the Self), though never stirring, is swifter than thought. The Devas (senses) never reached it, it walked before them. Though standing still, it overtakes the others who are running. Mâtarisvan (the wind, the moving spirit) bestows powers on it.

5. It stirs and it stirs not; it is far, and likewise near. It is inside of all this, and it is outside of all this.

6. And he who beholds all beings in the Self, and the Self in all beings, he never turns away from it.

7. When to a man who understands, the Self has become all things, what sorrow, what trouble can there be to him who once beheld that unity?

8. He (the Self) encircled all, bright, incorporeal, scatheless, without muscles, pure, untouched by evil; a seer, wise, omnipresent, self-existent, he disposed all things rightly for eternal years.

9. All who worship what is not real knowledge (good works) enter into blind darkness: those who delight in real knowledge enter, as it were, into greater darkness.

10. One thing, they say, is obtained from real knowledge; another, they say, from what is not knowledge. Thus we have heard from the wise who taught us this.

11. He who knows at the same time both knowledge and not-knowledge overcomes death through not-knowledge, and obtains immortality through knowledge.

12. All who worship what is not the true cause enter into blind darkness: those who delight in the true cause enter, as it were, into greater darkness.

13. One thing, they say, is obtained from knowledge of the cause; another, they say, from knowledge of what is not the cause. Thus we have heard from the wise who taught us this.

14. He who knows at the same time both the cause and the destruction (the perishable body), overcomes death by destruction (the perishable body), and obtains immortality through knowledge of the true cause.

15. The door of the True is covered with a golden disk. Open that, O Pûshan, that we may see the nature of the True.

16. O Pûshan, only seer, Yama (judge), Sûrya (sun), son of Pragâpati, spread thy rays and gather them! The light which is thy fairest form, I see it. I am what he is (viz., the person in the sun).

17. Breath to air, and to the immortal! Then this my body ends in ashes. Om! Mind, remember! Remember thy deeds! Mind, remember! Remember thy deeds!

18. Agni, lead us on to wealth (beatitude) by a good path, thou, O God, who knowest all things! Keep far from us crooked evil, and we shall offer thee the fullest praise! [1]

[1] This Upanishad, though apparently simple and intelligible, is in reality one of the most difficult to understand properly. Coming at the end of the Vâgasaneyi-samhitâ, in which the sacrifices and the hymns to be used by the officiating priests have been described, it begins by declaring that all has to be surrendered to the Lord. The name îs, "lord," is peculiar, as having a far more personal coloring than Atman, Self, or Brahman, the usual names given by the Upanishads to what is the object of the highest knowledge.

Next follows a permission to continue the performance of sacrifices, provided that all desires have been surrendered. And here occurs our first difficulty, which has perplexed ancient as well as modern commentators.

I shall try to justify my own translation. I hold that the Upanishad wishes to teach the uselessness by themselves of all good works, whether we call them sacrificial, legal, or moral, and yet, at the same time, to recognize, if not the necessity, at least the harmlessness of good works, provided they are performed without any selfish motives, without any desire of reward, but simply as a preparation for higher knowledge, as a means, in fact, of subduing all passions, and producing that serenity of mind without which man is incapable of receiving the highest knowledge. From that point of view the Upanishad may well say, Let a man wish to live here his appointed time; let him even perform all works. If only he knows that all must be surrendered to the Lord, then the work done by him will not cling to him. It will not work on and produce effect after effect, nor will it involve him in a succession of new births in which to enjoy the reward of his works, but it will leave him free to enjoy the blessings of the highest knowledge. It will have served as a preparation for that higher knowledge which the Upanishad imparts, and which secures freedom from further births.

# KATHA UPANISHAD

## FIRST ADHYÂYA

### FIRST VALLÎ

1. Vâgasravasa, desirous of heavenly reward, surrendered at a sacrifice all that he possessed. He had a son of the name of Nakiketas.

2. When the promised presents were being given to the priests, faith entered into the heart of Nakiketas, who was still a boy, and he thought:

3. "Unblessed, surely, are the worlds to which a man goes by giving as his promised present at a sacrifice cows which have drunk water, eaten hay, given their milk, and are barren."

4. He knowing that his father had promised to give up all that he possessed, and therefore his son also, said to his father: "Dear father, to whom wilt thou give me?"

He said it a second and a third time. Then the father replied angrily:

"I shall give thee unto Death."

[The father, having once said so, though in haste, had to be true to his word and to sacrifice his son.]

5. The son said: "I go as the first, at the head of many who have still to die; I go in the midst of many who are now dying. What will be the work of Yama, the ruler of the departed, which to-day he has to do unto me?[2]

---

[1] Anandagiri explains that the cows meant here are cows no longer able to drink, to eat, to give milk, and to calve.

[2] I translate these verses freely, *i.e.*, independently of the commentator; not that I ever despise the traditional interpretation which the commentators have preserved to us, but because I think that, after having examined it, we have a right to judge for ourselves. Sankara says that the son, having been addressed by his father full of anger, was sad, and said to himself: "Among many pupils I am the first, among many middling pupils I am the middlemost, but nowhere am I the last. Yet though I am such a good pupil, my father has said

6. "Look back how it was with those who came before; look forward how it will be with those who come hereafter. A mortal ripens like corn; like corn he springs up again."

[Nakiketas enters into the abode of Yama Vaivasvata, and there is no one to receive him. Thereupon one of the attendants of Yama is supposed to say:]

7. "Fire enters into the houses, when a Brâhmana enters as a guest. That fire is quenched by this peace-offering; bring water, O Vaivasvata! [3]

8. "A Brâhmana that dwells in the house of a foolish man, without receiving food to eat, destroys his hopes and expectations, his possessions, his righteousness, his sacred and his good deeds, and all his sons and cattle."

[Yama, returning to his house after an absence of three nights, during which time Nakiketas had received no hospitality from him, says:]

9. "O Brâhmana, as thou, a venerable guest, hast dwelt in my house three nights without eating, therefore choose now three boons. Hail to thee! and welfare to me!"

10. Nakiketas said: "O Death, as the first of the three boons I choose that Gautama, my father, be pacified, kind, and free from anger toward me; and that he may know me and greet me, when I shall have been dismissed by thee."

11. Yama said: "Through my favor Auddâlaki Aruni, thy father, will know thee, and be again toward thee as he was before. He shall sleep peacefully through the night, and free from anger, after having seen thee freed from the mouth of death."

12. Nakiketas said: "In the heaven-world there is no fear; thou art not there, O Death, and no one is afraid on account of old age. Leaving behind both hunger and thirst,

that he will consign me unto death. What duty has he to fulfil toward Yama which he means to fulfil to-day by giving me to him? There may be no duty; he may only have spoken in haste. Yet a father's word must not be broken." Having considered this, the son comforted his father, and exhorted him to behave like his forefathers, and to keep his word. I do not think this view of Sankara's could have been the view of the old poet.

[3] Vaivasvata, a name of Yama, the ruler of the departed. Water is the first gift to be offered to a stranger who claims hospitality.

and out of the reach of sorrow, all rejoice in the world of heaven.

13. "Thou knowest, O Death, the fire-sacrifice which leads us to heaven; tell it to me, for I am full of faith. Those who live in the heaven-world reach immortality; this I ask as my second boon."

14. Yama said: "I tell it thee, learn it from me, and when thou understandest that fire-sacrifice which leads to heaven, know, O Nakiketas, that it is the attainment of the endless worlds, and their firm support, hidden in darkness."

15. Yama then told him that fire-sacrifice, the beginning of all the worlds, and what bricks are required for the altar, and how many, and how they are to be placed. And Nakiketas repeated all as it had been told to him. Then Mrityu, being pleased with him, said again:

16. The generous, being satisfied, said to him: "I give thee now another boon; that fire-sacrifice shall be named after thee; take also this many-colored chain.

17. "He who has three times performed this Nâkiketa rite, and has been united with the three (father, mother, and teacher) and has performed the three duties (study, sacrifice, almsgiving) overcomes birth and death. When he has learnt and understood this fire, which knows or makes us know all that is born of Brahman, which is venerable and divine, then he obtains everlasting peace.

18. "He who knows the three Nâkiketa fires, and knowing the three, piles up the Nâkiketa sacrifice, he, having first thrown off the chains of death, rejoices in the world of heaven, beyond the reach of grief.

19. "This, O Nakiketas, is thy fire which leads to heaven, and which thou hast chosen as thy second boon. That fire all men will proclaim. Choose now, O Nakiketas, thy third boon."

20. Nakiketas said: "There is that doubt, when a man is dead — some saying, he is; others, he is not. This I should like to know, taught by thee: this is the third of my boons."

21. Death said: "On this point even the gods have doubted formerly; it is not easy to understand. That subject is subtle. Choose another boon, O Nakiketas; do not press me, and let me off that boon."

22. Nakiketas said: "On this point even the gods have doubted indeed, and thou, Death, hast declared it to be not easy to understand, and another teacher like thee is not to be found — surely no other boon is like unto this."

23. Death said: "Choose sons and grandsons who shall live a hundred years, herds of cattle, elephants, gold, and horses. Choose the wide abode of the earth, and live thyself as many harvests as thou desirest.

24. "If you can think of any boon equal to that, choose wealth and long life. Be king, Nakiketas, on the wide earth. I make thee the enjoyer of all desires.

25. "Whatever desires are difficult to attain among mortals, ask of them according to thy wish — these fair maidens with their chariots and musical instruments — such are indeed not to be obtained by men; be waited on by them whom I give to thee, but do not ask me about dying."

26. Nakiketas said: "These things last till to-morrow, O Death, for they wear out this vigor of all the senses. Even the whole of life is short. Keep thou thy horses, keep dance and song for thyself.

27. "No man can be made happy by wealth. Shall we possess wealth, when we see thee? Shall we live, as long as thou rulest? Only that boon which I have chosen is to be chosen by me.

28. "What mortal, slowly decaying here below, and knowing, after having approached them, the freedom from decay enjoyed by the immortals, would delight in a long life, after he has pondered on the pleasures which arise from beauty and love?

29. "No, that on which there is this doubt, O Death, tell us what there is in that great Hereafter. Nakiketas does not choose another boon but that which enters into the hidden world."

## Second Vallî

1. Death said: "The good is one thing, the pleasant another; these two, having different objects, chain a man. It is well with him who clings to the good; he who chooses the pleasant misses his end.

2. "The good and the pleasant approach man: the wise goes round about them and distinguishes them. Yea, the wise prefers the good to the pleasant, but the fool chooses the pleasant through greed and avarice.

3. "Thou, O Nakiketas, after pondering all pleasures that are or seem delightful, hast dismissed them all. Thou hast not gone into the road that leadeth to wealth, in which many men perish.

4. "Wide apart and leading to different points are these two — ignorance, and what is known as wisdom. I believe Nakiketas to be one who desires knowledge, for even many pleasures did not tear thee away.

5. "Fools dwelling in darkness, wise in their own conceit, and puffed up with vain knowledge, go round and round, staggering to and fro, like blind men led by the blind.

6. "The Hereafter never rises before the eyes of the careless child deluded by the delusion of wealth. 'This is the world,' he thinks, 'there is no other'; thus he falls again and again under my sway.

7. "He (the Self) of whom many are not even able to hear, whom many, even when they hear of him, do not comprehend; wonderful is a man, when found, who is able to teach him (the Self); wonderful is he who comprehends him, when taught by an able teacher.

8. "That Self, when taught by an inferior man, is not easy to be known, even though often thought upon; unless it be taught by another, there is no way to it, for it is inconceivably smaller than what is small.

9. "That doctrine is not to be obtained by argument, but when it is declared by another, then, O dearest, it is easy to understand. Thou hast obtained it now; thou art truly a

man of true resolve. May we have always an inquirer like thee!"

10. Nakiketas said: "I know that what is called a treasure is transient, for that eternal is not obtained by things which are not eternal. Hence the Nâkiketa fire-sacrifice has been laid by me first; then, by means of transient things, I have obtained what is not transient (the teaching of Yama)."

11. Yama said: "Though thou hadst seen the fulfilment of all desires, the foundation of the world, the endless rewards of good deeds, the shore where there is no fear, that which is magnified by praise, the wide abode, the rest, yet being wise thou hast with firm resolve dismissed it all.

12. "The wise who, by means of meditation on his Self, recognizes the Ancient, who is difficult to be seen, who has entered into the dark, who is hidden in the cave, who dwells in the abyss, as God, he indeed leaves joy and sorrow far behind.[2]

13. "A mortal who has heard this and embraced it, who has separated from it all qualities, and has thus reached the subtle Being, rejoices, because he has obtained what is a cause for rejoicing. The house of Brahman is open, I believe, O Nakiketas."

14. Nakiketas said: "That which thou seest as neither this nor that, as neither effect nor cause, as neither past nor future, tell me that."

15. Yama said: "That word or place which all the Vedas record, which all penances proclaim, which men desire when they live as religious students, that word I tell thee briefly — it is Om.

16. "That imperishable syllable means Brahman, that syllable means the highest (Brahman); he who knows that syllable, whatever he desires, is his.

17. "This is the best support; this is the highest sup-

[2] Yama seems here to propound the lower Brahman only, not yet the highest. Deva, God, can only be that as what the Old, *i.e.*, the Self in the heart, is to be recognized. It would therefore mean, he who finds God or the Self in his heart. See afterward, verse 21.

port; he who knows that support is magnified in the world of Bráhmâ.

18. " The knowing Self is not born, it dies not; it sprang from nothing, nothing sprang from it. The Ancient is unborn, eternal, everlasting; he is not killed, though the body is killed.

19. " If the killer thinks that he kills, if the killed thinks that he is killed, they do not understand; for this one does not kill, nor is that one killed.

20. " The Self, smaller than small, greater than great, is hidden in the heart of that creature. A man who is free from desires and free from grief sees the majesty of the Self by the grace of the Creator.

21. " Though sitting still, he walks far; though lying down, he goes everywhere. Who, save myself, is able to know that God who rejoices and rejoices not?

22. " The wise who knows the Self as bodiless within the bodies, as unchanging among changing things, as great and omnipresent, does never grieve.

23. " That Self can not be gained by the Veda, nor by understanding, nor by much learning. He whom the Self chooses, by him the Self can be gained. The Self chooses him (his body) as his own.

24. " But he who has not first turned away from his wickedness, who is not tranquil, and subdued, or whose mind is not at rest, he can never obtain the Self even by knowledge.

25. " Who then knows where he is, he to whom the Brahmans and Kshatriyas are, as it were, but food,[3] and death itself a condiment? "

## Third Vallî

1. " There are the two [4] drinking their reward in the dwelling on the highest summit (the ether in the heart). Those who know Brahman call them shade and light; like-

[3] In whom all disappears, and in whom even death is swallowed up.
[4] The two are explained as the higher and lower Brahman, the former being the light, the latter the shadow.

wise, those householders who perform the Trinâkiketa sacrifice.

2. "May we be able to master that Nâkiketa rite which is a bridge for sacrificers; also that which is the highest, imperishable Brahman for those who wish to cross over to the fearless shore.

3. "Know the Self to be sitting in the chariot, the body to be the chariot, the intellect (buddhi) the charioteer, and the mind the reins.

4. "The senses they call the horses, the objects of the senses their roads. When he (the Highest Self) is in union with the body, the senses, and the mind, then wise people call him the Enjoyer.

5. "He who has no understanding and whose mind (the reins) is never firmly held, his senses (horses) are unmanageable, like vicious horses of a charioteer.

6. "But he who has understanding and whose mind is always firmly held, his senses are under control, like good horses of a charioteer.

7. "He who has no understanding, who is unmindful and always impure, never reaches that place, but enters into the round of births.

8. "But he who has understanding, who is mindful and always pure, reaches indeed that place, from whence he is not born again.

9. "But he who has understanding for his charioteer, and who holds the reins of the mind, he reaches the end of his journey, and that is the highest place of Vishnu.

10. "Beyond the senses there are the objects, beyond the objects there is the mind, beyond the mind there is the intellect; the Great Self is beyond the intellect.

11. "Beyond the Great there is the Undeveloped, beyond the Undeveloped there is the Person (purusha). Beyond the Person there is nothing — this is the goal, the highest road.

12. "That Self is hidden in all beings and does not shine forth, but it is seen by subtle seers through their sharp and subtle intellect.

13. "A wise man should keep down speech and mind; he should keep them within the Self which is knowledge; he should keep knowledge within the Self which is the Great; and he should keep that (the Great) within the Self which is the Quiet.

14. "Rise, awake! having obtained your boons, understand them! The sharp edge of a razor is difficult to pass over; thus the wise say the path to the Self is hard.

15. "He who has perceived that which is without sound, without touch, without form, without decay, without taste, eternal, without smell, without beginning, without end, beyond the Great, and unchangeable, is freed from the jaws of death.

16. "A wise man who has repeated or heard the ancient story of Nakiketas told by Death is magnified in the world of Brahman.

17. "And he who repeats this greatest mystery in an assembly of Brahmans, or full of devotion at the time of the Srâddha sacrifice, obtains thereby infinite rewards."

SECOND ADHYÂYA

FOURTH VALLÎ

1. Death said: "The Self-existent pierced the openings of the senses so that they turn forward: therefore man looks forward, not backward into himself. Some wise man, however, with his eyes closed and wishing for immortality, saw the Self behind.

2. "Children follow after outward pleasures, and fall into the snare of wide-spread death. Wise men only, knowing the nature of what is immortal, do not look for anything stable here among things unstable.

3. "That by which we know form, taste, smell, sounds, and loving touches, by that also we know what exists besides. This is that which thou hast asked for.

4. "The wise, when he knows that that by which he perceives all objects in sleep or in waking is the great omnipresent Self, grieves no more.

5. "He who knows this living soul which eats honey perceives objects as being the Self, always near, the Lord of the past and the future, henceforward fears no more. This is that.

6. "He who knows him [5] who was born first from the brooding heat (for he was born before the water), who, entering into the heart, abides therein, and was perceived from the elements. This is that.

7. "He who knows Aditi also, who is one with all deities, who arises with Prana (breath or Hiranya-garbha), who, entering into the heart, abides therein, and was born from the elements. This is that.

8. "There is Agni (fire), the all-seeing, hidden in the two fire-sticks, well-guarded like a child in the womb by the mother, day after day to be adored by men when they awake and bring oblations. This is that.

9. "And that whence the sun rises, and whither it goes to set, there all the Devas are contained, and no one goes beyond. This is that.

10. "What is here visible in the world, the same is there, invisible in Brahman; and what is there, the same is here. He who sees any difference here between Brahman and the world, goes from death to death.

11. "Even by the mind this (Brahman) is to be obtained, and then there is no difference whatsoever. He goes from death to death who sees any difference here.

12. "The person (purusha), of the size of a thumb, stands in the middle of the Self (body), as lord of the past and the future, and henceforward fears no more. This is that.

13. "That person, of the size of a thumb, is like a light without smoke, lord of the past and the future, he is the same to-day and to-morrow. This is that.

14. "As rain-water that has fallen on a mountain-ridge runs down the rocks on all sides, thus does he, who sees a difference between qualities, run after them on all sides.

[5] The first manifestation of Brahman, commonly called Hiranya-garbha, which springs from the tapas of Brahman. Afterward only water and the rest of the elements become manifested.

15. "As pure water poured into pure water remains the same, thus, O Gautama, is the Self of a thinker who knows."

## FIFTH VALLÎ

1. "There is a town with eleven [6] gates belonging to the Unborn (Brahman), whose thoughts are never crooked. He who approaches it grieves no more, and liberated from all bonds of ignorance becomes free. This is that.

2. "He (Brahman) is the swan (sun), dwelling in the bright heaven; he is the Vasu (air), dwelling in the sky; he is the sacrificer (fire), dwelling on the hearth; he is the guest (Soma), dwelling in the sacrificial jar; he dwells in men, in gods (vara), in the sacrifice (rita), in heaven; he is born in the water, on earth, in the sacrifice (rita), on the mountains; he is the True and the Great.

3. "He (Brahman) it is who sends up the breath (prana), and who throws back the breath (apâna). All the Devas (senses) worship him, the adorable (or the dwarf), who sits in the center.

4. "When that incorporated (Brahman), who dwells in the body, is torn away and freed from the body, what remains then? This is that.

5. "No mortal lives by the breath that goes up and by the breath that goes down. We live by another, in whom these two repose.

6. "Well then, O Gautama, I shall tell thee this mystery, the old Brahman, and what happens to the Self, after reaching death.

7. "Some enter the womb in order to have a body, as organic beings, others go into inorganic matter, according to their work and according to their knowledge.

8. "He, the highest Person, who is awake in us while we are asleep, shaping one lovely sight after another — that indeed is the Bright; that is Brahman; that alone is called immortal. All worlds are contained in it, and no one goes beyond. This is that.

[6] Seven apertures in the head, the navel, two below, and the one at the top of the head through which the Self escapes.

9. "As the one fire, after it has entered the world, though one, becomes different according to whatever it burns, thus the one Self within all things becomes different, according to whatever it enters, and exists also without.

10. "As the one air, after it has entered the world, though one, becomes different according to whatever it enters, thus the one Self within all things becomes different, according to whatever it enters, and exists also without.

11. "As the sun, the eye of the whole world, is not contaminated by the external impurities seen by the eyes, thus the one Self within all things is never contaminated by the misery of the world, being himself without.

12. "There is one ruler, the Self within all things, who makes the one form manifold. The wise who perceive him within their Self, to them belongs eternal happiness, not to others.

13. "There is one eternal thinker, thinking non-eternal thought, who, though one, fulfils the desires of many. The wise who perceive him within their Self, to them belongs eternal peace, not to others.

14. "They perceive that highest indescribable pleasure, saying, This is that. How then can I understand it? Has it its own light, or does it reflect light?

15. "The sun does not shine there, nor the moon and the stars, nor these lightnings, and much less this fire. When he shines, everything shines after him; by his light all this is lighted."

### Sixth Vallî

1. "There is that ancient tree,[7] whose roots grow upward and whose branches grow downward; that indeed is called the Bright; that is called Brahman; that alone is called the Immortal. All worlds are contained in it, and no one goes beyond. This is that.

2. "Whatever there is, the whole world, when gone forth from the Brahman, trembles in its breath. That Brahman

[7] The fig-tree which sends down its branches so that they strike root and form new stems, one tree growing into a complete forest.

is a great terror, like a drawn sword. Those who know it become immortal.

3. "From terror of Brahman fire burns, from terror the sun burns, from terror Indra and Vayu, and Death, as the fifth, run away.

4. "If a man could not understand it before the falling asunder of his body, then he has to take body again in the worlds of creation.

5. "As in a mirror, so Brahman may be seen clearly here in this body; as in a dream, in the world of the Fathers; as in the water, he is seen about in the world of the Gandharvas; as in light and shade, in the world of Bráhmâ.

6. "Having understood that the senses are distinct (from the Atman), and that their rising and setting (their waking and sleeping) belong to them in their distinct existence, and not to the Atman, a wise man grieves no more.

7. "Beyond the senses is the mind; beyond the mind is the highest created Being; higher than that Being is the Great Self; higher than the Great, the highest Undeveloped.

8. "Beyond the Undeveloped is the Person, the all-pervading and entirely imperceptible. Every creature that knows him is liberated, and obtains immortality.

9. "His form is not to be seen; no one beholds him with the eye. He is imagined by the heart, by wisdom, by the mind. Those who know this are immortal.

10. "When the five instruments of knowledge stand still together with the mind, and when the intellect does not move, that is called the highest state.

11. "This, the firm holding back of the senses, is what is called Yoga. He must be free from thoughtlessness then, for Yoga comes and goes.

12. "He (the Self) can not be reached by speech, by mind, or by the eye. How can it be apprehended except by him who says: ' He is '?

13. "By the words ' He is,' is he to be apprehended, and by admitting the reality of both the invisible Brahman and the visible world, as coming from Brahman. When he has

been apprehended by the words 'He is,' then his reality reveals itself.

14. " When all desires that dwell in his heart cease, then the mortal becomes immortal, and obtains Brahman.

15. " When all the ties of the heart are severed here on earth, then the mortal becomes immortal — here ends the teaching. [8]

16. " There are a hundred and one arteries of the heart; one of them penetrates the crown of the head. Moving upward by it, a man at his death reaches the Immortal; the other arteries serve for departing in different directions.

17. " The Person not larger than a thumb, the inner Self, is always settled in the heart of men. Let a man draw that Self forth from his body with steadiness, as one draws the pith from a reed. Let him know that Self as the Bright, as the Immortal; yes, as the Bright, as the Immortal."

18. Having received this knowledge taught by Death and the whole rule of Yoga (meditation), Nakiketa became free from passion and death, and obtained Brahman. Thus it will be with another also who knows thus what relates to the Self.

19. May he protect us both! May he enjoy us both! May we acquire strength together! May our knowledge become bright! May we never quarrel! Om! Peace! peace! peace! Hari, Om!

[8] The teaching of the Vedanta extends so far and no further. What follows has reference, according to the commentator, not to him who knows the highest Brahman, for he becomes Brahman at once and migrates no more; but to him who does not know the highest Brahman fully, and therefore migrates to the Brahmaloka, receiving there the reward for his partial knowledge and for his good works.

## YAMA AND NAKIKETAS.

*Yama, God of Death, teaches his Dark Wisdom to the youth vowed to his service.*

# THE TEACHING OF SANDILYA [1]

## FROM THE KHANDOGYA UPANISHAD

1. All this is Bráhmâ.[2] Let a man meditate on that visible world as beginning, ending and breathing [3] in it (the Bráhmâ).

Now man is a creature of will. According to what his will is in this world, so will he be when he has departed this life. Let him therefore have this will and belief.

2. The intelligent, whose body is spirit, whose form is light, whose thoughts are true, whose nature is like ether (omnipresent and invisible), from whom all works, all desires, all sweet odors and tastes proceed; he who embraces all this, who never speaks, and is never surprised,

3. He is my self within the heart, smaller than a corn of rice, smaller than a corn of barley, smaller than a mustard-seed, smaller than a canary-seed or the kernel of a canary-seed. He also is my self within the heart, greater than the earth, greater than the sky, greater than heaven, greater than all these worlds.

4. He from whom all works, all desires, all sweet odors and tastes proceed, who embraces all this, who never speaks and who is never surprised, he, my self within the heart, is that Bráhmâ. When I shall have departed from hence, I shall obtain him (that Self). He who has this faith [4] has no doubt; thus said Sandilya, yea, thus he said.

1 This is the fourteenth Khanda or chapter of the third part of the Khandogya Upanishad. It forms one of the most quoted teachings of Brahmanism.

2 That is, everything is God.

3 Galân is explained by *ga*, born, *la*, absorbed, and *an*, breathing. It is an artificial term, but fully recognized by the Vedanta school, and always explained in this manner.

4 Or he who has faith, and no doubt, will obtain this.

## BRÁHMÁ, OR THE UNIVERSAL SOUL [5]

### 1.

This universe is Bráhmá's Self!
   A part of him — these creatures all!
In him their birth, they live in him,
   And into him they end withal!
The mortal ever toils and works,
   And as he sows upon this earth,
In virtue's soil or ways of sin,
   So reaps he in a future birth!

### 2.

He is Life — Intelligence pure!
   He is Truth and he is Light!
His soul pervades the universe,
   Like ether — escapes our mortal sight!
From him alone all works proceed,
   All wishes and all feelings spring,
Serene and calm, he never speaks,
   But in himself holds everything!

### 3.

He is the Self within my heart,
   The Soul that lives and dwells within,
Smaller than the smallest seed,
   Or kernel of smallest grain!
He is the Self within my heart,
   Greater than the earth and sky,
Greater far than all the worlds,
   Greater than the heaven on high!

[5] This is a modern versified rendering of the preceding "Teaching of Sandilya." It is by the Hindu poet and scholar R. C. Dutt.

### 4.

From him alone all works proceed,
　　All wishes and all feelings spring,
Serene and calm, he never speaks,
　　But in himself holds everything!
He is the Self within my heart,
　　He is Bráhmâ! — holding all,
And when I leave this world — to him
　　Will flee my liberated soul!

This is the end of this publication.

Any remaining blank pages are for our book binding requirements and are blank on purpose.

To search thousands of interesting publications like this one, please remember to visit our website at:

http://www.kessinger.net

Printed in the USA
CPSIA information can be obtained
at www.ICGtesting.com
LVHW081657240823
756121LV00018B/29

9 781169 250734